Praise for
Jesus the Forgotten Feminist

Geraghty has brought his forensic skills as a former District Court Judge and (his) impressive research of the primary sources to produce a myth-busting wake-up call for the Church.

Theologically literate, historically well researched and dynamite in its conclusion. Gergaghty blasts away centuries of entrenched patriarchy and misogyny to show the churches, in particular his own Catholic church, have betrayed their founder in the status they deny women.

– **Paul Bongiorno,**
veteran political journalist and commentator

Geraghty's persuasive and attractive description of *Jesus the forgotten feminist* is underpinned by extensive scholarship... Contemporary Catholic feminists who have long argued a position like Geraghty's will welcome this book, as will the general reader... Geraghty's conclusion is that those who restored and still maintain pre-Jesus Christ misogyny have departed grievously from Jesus' teachings. This conclusion will be welcomed by many and vigorously resisted by others.

– **Susan Ryan, AO**

The living Christian tradition preserves the rich heritage of a past that has meant so much to countless multitudes over the centuries. The great strength of this tradition is that it also has within it the power and resources to break open the prison doors of the past and present to allow something new and fresh to appear. Chris Geraghty has allowed the women who were so important in Jesus' ministry, but pushed onto the sidelines by his male followers, to regain their truly prominent position in the gospel story. Now, off the sidelines into the centre of the field, I expect them to find their voices.

– **Father Neil Brown, Australian theologian**

Published in Australia by
Garratt Publishing
32 Glenvale Crescent
Mulgrave, VIC 3170
www.garrattpublishing.com.au

Copyright in this work remains the property of the contributing authors.

Copyright © Chris Geraghty 2018

All rights reserved. Except as proviwded by the Australian copyright law, no part of this book may be reproduced in any way without permission in writing from the publisher.

Cover Design by Lynne Muir
Text Design by Lynne Muir
Edited by Nick Mattiske & Juliette Hughes-Norwood
Cover image 'Do Not Hold Onto Me', He Qi © 2013 all rights reserved, www.heqiart.com
Author Photograph © Adele Geraghty 2018

Scripture taken from the *Revised Standard Version*, Grand Rapids: Zondervan, 1971. Scriptures marked JB are taken from the *The Jerusalem Bible* © 1966 by Darton Longman & Todd Ltd and Doubleday and Company Ltd.

All rights reserved.

ISBN 9781925073478

Cataloguing in Publication information for this title is available from the National Library of Australia.

www.nla.gov.au

The authors and publisher gratefully acknowledge the permission granted to reproduce the copyright material in this book. Every effort has been made to trace copyright holders and to obtain their permission for the use of copyright material.

The publisher apologises for any errors or omissions in the above list and would be grateful if notified of any corrections that should be incorporated in future reprints or editions of this book.

JESUS
the forgotten feminist

CHRIS GERAGHTY

garratt
PUBLISHING

Contents

INTRODUCTION 3

CHAPTER ONE
Looking Through a Wide-Angle Lens 7

CHAPTER TWO
A Fundamental Question 15

CHAPTER THREE
Prospecting in a Paddock of Theology 19

CHAPTER FOUR
A First Century Portrait of a Preacher 29

CHAPTER FIVE
**The Backdrop to a Drama
Jesus' Message of a Kingdom** 44

CHAPTER SIX
A Woman's World at the Time of Jesus
The Cultural Setting 62

Women in Public Life...65
The Synagogue and Ritual Purity Prescriptions.............70
The Temple in King David's City..................................73
Adam and Eve embedded in the Jewish Psyche............77
The Jewish Wisdom Literature 83
Marriage and Divorce 92
Female Education 97
The Lot of a Female Slave..98
In Summary 99

CHAPTER SEVEN
'Not Counting Women and Children' 101

CHAPTER EIGHT
Jesus' Female Followers.......................................107

CHAPTER NINE
Jesus' Close Encounters with the Opposite Sex.................114

A Woman Caught in the Act..114
The Foreign Woman at the Well..................................118
Two Sisters at Home with Jesus 122
A Female Admirer 130
The Syrophoenician Woman.......................................138
The Woman Ritually and Permanently Impure............142
The Might of Widows 143
Chaos in the Synagogue...146
An Ambitious Mother 149

CHAPTER TEN
The Women of the Passion 160

CHAPTER ELEVEN
Any Women Around the Table of the Lord? 168

CHAPTER TWELVE
The Resurrection Narratives 181

CHAPTER THIRTEEN
The Post-Resurrection Infancy Narratives 194

    A Lifeline for Jesus 195
    Women of the Infancy Narratives 204

CHAPTER FOURTEEN
Telling It How It Is 221

What Say You, Christine de Pizan? 229

Bibliography 230

Gospel References 232

Note:
The author has indicated with an asterisk (*) any RSV passage of scripture that he has modified somewhat in an attempt to convey its meaning more directly or, in a few instances, to present in his own words the nature of a particular scriptural interaction, or to record an occasional explanatory note within a quotation.

Introduction

Not another book about Jesus! Haven't we had more than enough by now? There must be thousands of them out there floating about in libraries and bookshops. What more can there be to say?

I am persuaded that in my dementia years I might have found something interesting, maybe even important, to say about Jesus: about his relationship with women and about their involvement in his life and mission.

From my primary school years with the nuns at Neutral Bay (apart from a few wasted years of pious devotion to an effeminate self-absorbed figure we called 'The Sacred Heart') I accepted without question an image of Jesus as a man's man – travelling with his mates, whip in hand among the traders and financiers in Jerusalem – stoical, blunt, fearless and fearsome. He hadn't even pretended to suffer patiently those religious fools who were in charge of the show. He had bashed up the bankers in the Temple precincts and abused the religious leaders and theologians. The Jesus I knew had been in control of his feelings and his urges – a natural, fine-tuned celibate, relaxed with his mates on the golf course but aloof in the presence of women; always on his guard, as every Jewish young man had been taught to be (and as the institution had trained me to be) at least until the age of forty.

As far as I was concerned, apart from his virgin mother, women had not loomed large in Jesus' life, though I acknowledged there had been some women hovering at the fringes of his world. Mary Magdalene comes to mind. He had certainly been respectful to the various females he had happened to come in contact with, but his world and his work had been crowded out by men – his team of male disciples and an inner group of apostles had defined and confined his world, while male intellectuals and officials who had sought to undermine his message had finally brought him down.

When it came to establishing a church, for a long time I simply accepted that Jesus had himself laid the foundations of the institution to which I belonged by birth, and that he had commissioned men – men only – to take control and lead his followers to the promised land: Peter and the other apostles, male disciples and mates on the road. The society Jesus had inhabited and the church he had founded were male dominated – the message and all that flowed from it (the teaching, the preaching, the rules and regulations, and the liturgical celebrations) was unquestionably men's business.

My recent interest in Christian misogyny was initially sparked by what has emerged in the past decades as official doctrine from the Vatican. A Polish pope had forbidden his followers to discuss the burning issue of female ordination. As far as he was concerned, the issue was off the agenda and contrary to the clear wishes of the founder. Not a polite request, not a gentle invitation – a heavy-handed order from above. The subject was not pornographic. It wasn't terrorist talk. The role of women in a modern society and the ordination of women were perfectly legitimate topics of conversation around any dinner table, in the pub or for the ladies in the knitting club – except if you were a Roman Catholic who happened to support their inclusion among the ranks of the clergy.

Then Cardinal Josef Ratzinger, as head of the most powerful department in the Vatican, before he became pope, tried to frighten the troops by announcing to an incredulous world that the issue has been decided definitively, almost infallibly. Women couldn't ever be priests or bishops, or – heaven forbid – a pope.

And Pope Francis, for all his bonhomie and friendly pastoral touch, also informed those who were still listening that the door to the female ordination room was closed. No entry! But exactly what was he telling us? Closed forever? Padlocked? And who were holding the keys to the cellar? A cabal of misogynist bachelors?

I am curious to find out what was behind this closed door. The magical world of Narnia? A treasure chest of theological jewels and scholarly tomes, of edifying thoughts as the papacy would have us all believe, or funny masks, musty drapes and a collection of religious bric-à-brac? What were the real reasons behind this lofty intransigence? What did these elderly gentlemen over in the Vatican believe was the basis for their Church's long-standing tradition? If it was Jesus' clear wish, we had something to talk about, and I wanted to contribute to the conversation.

From where I stood, these modern papal celibates were the living, breathing repository of a long line of misogyny that contaminated the minds of influential Christian leaders such as Tertullian from the second century and Jerome from the fourth century; Augustine of Hippo, John Chrysostom, Innocent III, Bonaventure, Thomas Aquinas – popes, monks, bishops, theologians.

In the late fourth century, at the Synod of Laodicea, a team of local bishops decided that women had to be kept well away from the altar (*canon 22*). Subsequent teams of important episcopal celibates repeated the ruling – at the Synod of Nîmes at the end of the fourth century, at the Synod of Nantes in the seventh century and again in the eighth century at the Synod of Aachen where the assembled bishops decided that admitting women even to the lower ranks of the hierarchy was not allowed because it was 'indecent' and contrary to apostolic church order.

At the end of the fifth century, a furious Pope Gelasius wrote to the bishops of Lucania:

> As we have learnt to our anger, such contempt for the divine truths has set in that even women, it has been reported, serve at the holy altars. And everything that is exclusively entrusted to the service of men has been carried out by the sex that has no right to do it.

The minutes of the Reform Synod of Paris from the early ninth century went on to record:

> In some provinces it happens that women press around the altar, touch the holy vessels, hand the clerics the priestly vestments, and even dispense the body and blood of the Lord to the people. This is shameful and must cease ... No doubt such customs have arisen because of the carelessness and negligence of the bishops.

Shameful, indecent, offensive, unreasonable practices involving women must have been breaking out in plague proportions. The local authorities and the pope in Rome had to step in and crush these evil practices. The heavy hand of authority was raised to exclude the women. The Polish pope was only continuing the ancient tradition of the institution.

The intransigence of our recent popes prodded me into action. I wanted to see if I could trace the development of the Christian tradition of misogyny. Could I discover (with any degree of certainty after all this time) what Jesus' thoughts were on the subject? Who was he? What did he say? How would we ever know? Did he set out to establish a church? And to institute a new line of male priesthood? Did he prioritise men over women? Did he ordain anyone at all? How confined are we as believers by what appears in the gospels, or by what we accept as our traditions? Is there no room to move, or are we doomed to remain imprisoned in the past?

The popes drove me back to the sources – that's their job – to Jesus and his friends, his female friends, to the gospels and to the interpretation of a series of gospel passages and traditions, to the letters of St Paul, to the pastoral epistles and beyond, into the world of the early Church. Reluctantly I came to the conclusion that when it came to the place of women within the primitive churches, Paul of Tarsus and the early Church Fathers had drifted away from the path Jesus had laid out, so that the prophetic wishes of Jesus, in so far as we can identify them, have never been properly explored. It is clear from the gospels that women were important in Jesus' life and mission, with an importance that has been denied them in the life of the church.

It is inevitable that until it has learnt to eat humble pie, to read the signs of the times and take up again the message and values of Jesus, the Church will continue to pay the price for its intransigence. I have no doubt the day will come when women will occupy their rightful place among the followers of Jesus. There was a time when it was unheard of that a woman would possess a driver's licence or drink in a public bar. It was once unthinkable that reasonable, rational men would grant the vote to their mothers and wives, to grannies and girl-friends. Now it's difficult to understand why some clubs exclude women from their inner sanctums, why after heated, irrational public discussion, the old brigade continue to refuse them entry – then capitulate and finally accept the inevitable.

Therefore I am confident that some future pope and his advisers will eventually be awakened from their long sleep by some angel's kiss, rub their bleary eyes, take the messenger's hand and accompany her into the twenty-first century. Though I am almost eighty, I am hoping I will live to see it. Until then, the Vatican bachelors hold the keys and hold the future of our church.

Now let's get on with it. But in all conscience, I cannot set you free to roam around inside my biblical world without paying a special tribute to the two people who have assisted me in giving birth to this book.

I first met Neil Brown when we were serving time together in the seminary. We were ordained together in St Mary's Cathedral in Sydney, travelled overseas together to further our religious education and to see the world. We have been friends, close friends, for over fifty years and without being in any way responsible for the heresies and irreverences you might find in the following pages, he accompanied me as my research progressed, made his gentle comments and suggestions, asked questions, and when I was down on fuel, encouraged me to continue. Thanks, Neil.

Finally, in the autumn of my years, my life-partner and mother of our two boys Patrice and Pascal allowed me the time and the space to research, to visit libraries, to spread my papers and books far and wide, in every room of the house, on every table and vacant surface. Without a word of complaint, she put up with me getting up in the early hours of the morning to capture a passing thought in words, for fear a little gem might escape. Then in the end (and honestly, without much interest in the material) she went through my final draft meticulously with her red pen – correcting grammar and spelling errors, tightening sentences, making suggestions. I hope she can recognise her hand in the finished product. Thank you, Adele.

CHAPTER ONE

Looking Through a Wide-Angle Lens

The story told between the covers of this book is a tragic one for all true believers.

Such hope turned to ashes, and so quickly. A dazzling vision for the future reduced to a grey monotone within a few generations. A brave new world undermined and forgotten.

The Jesus of the gospels never drew up a policy statement on women to distance himself from all forms of misogyny, to abrogate an anti-feminist use of the Adam and Eve myth, to assert that women were equal to men in status and importance, that they were full members of his kingdom movement with all its rights and privileges, that they were to be involved in ministry and free to act with his authority and in his name. He never declared that within his salvation movement women were to be forever inferior to men as they were in the wider community during his lifetime, subject to their husbands and fathers, and reduced to silence in the prayer gatherings within the synagogues.

But then again, Jesus never announced a policy about men either, about sex's purpose and frequency, or about the environment, climate change, war, wealth, capital and banking, slavery, or about liturgical worship. No dogmatic formulae, as far as we are told, fell from his lips. Nothing about Adam and Eve, or original sin, or about the filth of sexual concourse. No rules and regulations. All that came later – with Paul of Tarsus and with the faceless author of the pastoral epistles, with Tertullian and Jerome, with popes, bishops, abbots and theologians. Jesus was not a philosopher, or a theologian. Certainly not a lawyer, or a businessman, a politician, a spin doctor, a union organiser or an expert in administration. All these activities were left to others who would be called on to erect structures and barriers around the message of the kingdom. Jesus was the visionary, the message-man sent by God to show the way.

When it came to all the other issues, including the general status and role of women and their place within the Christian communities, in so far as an answer to those questions is governed by the mind of Jesus, the relevant principles and values have had to be teased out from his sayings and from the description of events as recorded some decades later. The implications rumbling about under the texts have had to be made explicit, and God knows, theologians and primates of the Church have been hard at work over the centuries. Even now, as always, passages have to be carefully scrutinised, assessed and interpreted. The rich vein of subtext in the gospels has to be identified. We have to be ready to accept that some passages have been ignored in the past, or misinterpreted, exaggerated, given more importance than they can bear – or less. These passages have been viewed in the past within a devotional context. Blinded by ignorance or prejudice or by a desire to hang on to power, Christians have failed to appreciate their obvious political (even radical) weight.

As Jesus travelled about, in and out of people's lives and homes, he made frequent contact with women, meeting with them, speaking to them, preaching to them, sharing secrets, encouraging, forgiving and healing them. Some of these women became members of his group of followers and were important witnesses of what Jesus had said and done in and around Galilee and on the road to Jerusalem. They were witnesses in the Temple city itself, were maybe also at a last farewell supper, perhaps in the garden of Gethsemane, certainly when he was on the cross and throughout the period of his post-Resurrection appearances.

Apart from those women who were Jesus' regular companions during his public ministry and at the time of his death, other women came into his life, briefly, unexpectedly, and quietly exited stage left, never to be heard of again. The much-married Samaritan woman was one. And the sinner (*not* Mary of Magdala) who had washed and oiled his feet at the house of Simon the Pharisee was another. The gospel authors mentioned others. We should watch carefully to see how he related to them and how they treated him.

The movie that the gospel producers have projected onto our religious screens tells the life-story of a Jesus who did not steer clear of females of any age, even those with suspect reputation. He was not avoiding them or even, as the law and custom of the land required him to do, strictly controlling their contact with him. He engaged with them in ways that were unconventional, even illegal, for the times. He engaged with women in ways that would eventually be strongly advised against by church authorities and spiritual directors monitoring the behaviour of celibate clergy and members of religious orders who rejoice in, (or suffer each day the torment of) their vows of chastity.

Jesus was not on his guard, protecting his virtue, safeguarding his reputation and preserving his ritual purity. When he was out and about in public, he was walking the streets, eating and drinking with publicans and sinners. He was not 'taking Prudence by the hand', as seminarians were advised to do in my day. It was not his way to be forever vigilant, screening his followers, making sure they were male members of his club and no threat to his sexuality. Jesus was out there – open, available, fully present, aware, ready to engage; challenging and confronting the established bureaucrats, official secretaries, clerks, religious leaders. He was always inviting his listeners to respond generously. He was never on the defensive and welcomed anyone, including the women who were going out to him with trust and personal warmth.

The goldmine of references to women in the gospel accounts of Jesus' life is remarkable, especially when compared to the literature of the day, to the works of Josephus, of Philo, or the Book of Proverbs, for example. In these more or less contemporary works, women were mostly invisible. When they did appear, they generally attracted only a passing mention, or else were notorious for their beauty, their sexual attractiveness, or for some noteworthy wickedness. It is different in the gospels.

All four gospels frequently make reference to women in the life of Jesus, and Luke's Gospel is a stand-out. When we read the literature, what is peculiar is that of all the other groups of people with whom Jesus was regularly in contact – Pharisees, priests, scribes, Sadducees, tax collectors, guests at table, even the apostles – none of them appear to have included women as members of their group. Their troops were made up of men. In the gospel literature, where events that do not involve Jesus are narrated (the infancy narratives, for example, involving shepherds and kings, or accounts of feasts, the synagogue, crowd scenes in which Jesus is questioned or challenged), women are almost absent. Apart from an occasional reference here and there, women pass unnoticed. We presume they were there in the picture, but when they were away from Jesus, they hovered in the ether like ghosts, while men, alone or in the company of other men, were strutting about on the Palestinian stage.

Apart from the women in and around Jesus' group, there were also a few cameo roles for other women in the gospels – the female slave who accosted Peter for being with Jesus the Galilean; the wife of Pilate who had had a troubling dream about Jesus; the daughter of Herodias whom Josephus identified as Salome, dancing her heart out to pleasure the king and his courtiers. These passages support what common sense would suggest – that women were present in the society of the times, playing their minor part in the social fabric of the day, in the royal court, around the perimeter of the Sanhedrin, for example, but not graced with a speaking role.

The authors of the gospels did not avoid the fact that Jesus' behaviour was contrary to the custom of the day and, as we will see, often offended both Jewish customs and the strict prohibitions of the Mosaic Law. He was portrayed in the early Christian literature quite simply as going about his business, living his life as a layman, dealing with people, giving little heed to the petty restrictions of the law, paying no attention to what might be said by way of criticism.

He was deeply religious, but not what one might call a strictly 'orthodox', law-abiding Jew. A non-conformist. A liberal Jew, proud of his heritage, but free of scruples, untroubled by crazy legalism and religious obsessions. And it should be unnecessary to observe that he was not a bishop, or a priest, or a Catholic; and of course, not a Roman Catholic cardinal of reactionary persuasion.

Jesus' primary message centred on a kingdom, the Kingdom of Heaven – a kingdom which was peopled by sinners, by the lost and the lame, the blind and the deaf, by children and by women – a kingdom where everyone was equal and the first were last and the servant of all. A vision in which people loved one another and in which it didn't matter whether you were black or white, Jew or Gentile, young or old, slave or free, male or female. Jesus had appeared in an isolated region of the world preaching revolution.

> There is neither Jew nor Greek, slave or free, male and female – for all are one in Christ Jesus (Gal 3:28)*
>
> Here (in our community) there cannot be Greek or Jew, circumcised and uncircumcised, barbarian, Scythian, slave, free man, but Christ is all, and in all. (Col 3:11)
>
> For by one Spirit we were all baptised into one body – Jews and Greeks, slaves and free – and all were made to drink on one Spirit. (1 Cor 12:13)

A kingdom of heaven on earth. In the life of Jesus and in his kingdom, women were front and centre – female friends and companions; female admirers and camp-followers who worked with him; women in need who sought him out for help for themselves and the members of their families. He consistently treated them with dignity and respect. As we will see, he listened to them and communicated directly with them. Not once did he condemn a woman, as he did the Pharisees, scribes and Sadducees. Women were not the object of reproach, much less of bitter condemnation. Jesus treated women as friends and enjoyed their company. Stepping outside the square, shocking the conservatives and traditionalists: surprising, challenging, generating gossip, horrifying. It must have been a heady experience for a woman to be in his company and part of his team, observing the reactions of the crowd and especially of the Jewish officials.

In the gospel narratives, women are also depicted as exemplars of the level of faith and commitment Jesus was seeking from his followers. While challenging the quality of the twelve's faith and criticising their woodenness, Jesus was ready to praise the faith of the women he met casually in the street – even pagan women. The faith of the female members of Jesus' entourage received special attention from the composers of the gospels, who were almost certainly all males.

Women were accepted, without comment, as followers of Jesus, as his disciples. This presentation of women in the life and work of Jesus was radical and counter-cultural in a Jewish society where women were expected to be submissive and largely invisible in public places.

Contrary to the legal practice of the time, women were depicted by the gospel writers as trustworthy witnesses of the crucial gospel events – the suffering, death and resurrection of the Lord. They were there on the scene when the generals had deserted the battlefield. The female witnesses were entrusted with delivering the message of the Resurrection, and though initially not believed, their evidence eventually proved true. Jesus' female followers are presented to us as reliable messengers and authorised prophets.

We can see from the early records that after Jesus' death and disappearance, women continued to be involved, at least for a time, at the centre of the Christian communities – as missionaries, servants or deaconesses, prophetesses, teachers – participating in the life and work of the community and active within its liturgical prayer meetings. But quite rapidly their involvement began to fade: as Christians came into contact with the world outside Palestine and Paul began to institutionalise the visionary movement Jesus had launched and to develop authority structures. Paul also began to construct his theological insights around Jesus and the Church and it was then that serious fault lines emerged.

Modifications began to appear in the warp and weft of the movement. The kingdom preaching that had flavoured Jesus' message would disappear with him. Instead of looking to the future, to the coming of the kingdom, the leaders and authorities very soon began to look back over their shoulders to the past, to preserve their traditions, to conserve what they had been taught, to establish structures, ministries, rules and regulations, and lines of authority.

The immensely flexible symbol of a new kingdom, the new world order, so rich and polychromatic on Jesus' palette, would be replaced by the image of an institution – a church, or churches, founded among local communities. The inhabitants of the kingdom, the marginalised and fringe-dwellers, lepers, tax collectors, the invisible riff-raff (and women), some with highly suspicious reputations, would be replaced by Jewish and pagan converts, those who had been baptised and who attended the prayer meetings, with those who believed in Jesus and who formed part of the institution and who agreed to abide by its regulations and accept its faith formulae. The prominent, prophetic women were replaced with women who were submissive, who knew their places and who would remain silent in the gatherings.

Christians would see changes occurring – the vision disappearing and Jesus' dream (of a future kingdom where women could live with the same dignity and importance as their counterparts) becoming an ugly nightmare. Within a few generations women had become the enemy: daughters of Eve, the primeval temptress and the gateway to Hell.

When Jesus' visionary movement emerged from its homeland at the far-flung regions of the Roman Empire, it hit rough territory around the borders of the Mediterranean – Greco-Roman culture, pagan beliefs, many strange gods, wild Eastern cults, powerful Gnostic sects – a cauldron of beliefs and practices to contaminate the pure message of the preacher-man. Against these pressures, the kingdom message of Jesus, his policy of inclusion and equality, love and acceptance, would have little chance of survival in its pure form. His newly minted attitude to women would be just one of the many items of collateral damage.

CHAPTER TWO

A Fundamental Question

After one of the sessions of the Second Vatican Council, Bishop Tom McCabe from Wollongong and Bishop John Norton of Bathurst were strolling down the nave of St Peter's Basilica, chatting away as they made their way out into the sunshine. They passed through the majestic bronze doors and paused at the top of the marble staircase, looking down over the vast square where thousands of bishops and archbishops were standing around, some dragging on a cigarette, gossiping in groups, all glorious in their full-length robes of episcopal reds and purples. The Italian sun was sparkling on a patchwork quilt of gaudy colours. Johnny Norton had come from Ireland to Australia as a young priest and had been the bishop of a sunburnt country diocese for over thirty years. And Tom was not much younger. He was a man's man, a laconic, no-nonsense Aussie prelate who was by nature uncomfortable in his Renaissance gear.

Norton looked down across the assembled crowd (all men of course), turned to his mate and observed dryly in his Irish-Aussie drawl,

'Looks like a paddock of Paterson's curse.'

Paterson's curse is a colourful purple weed that grows prolifically in paddocks around rural Australia and has resisted all scientific attempts at eradication.

Back in Wollongong, after the Council, Bishop Tom had received a respectful letter from two laymen of his little coastal diocese asking him to establish a diocesan lay advisory council – as had been recommended by the international collection of bishops and cardinals who had spent long, boring hours in Rome during the Council. Bishop McCabe called his clerical team of advisers together to draft a suitable response: Monsignor Dignan, a conservative Irish cleric who for years had enjoyed the dignity of the clerical state and the quiet life it delivered; Father Peter Moore, a middle-aged cleric; Father Ferdie Fulendorf, a practical, pastoral man from the deep south of the diocese; and the recently appointed administrator of the Cathedral, my friend and classmate Father Michael Bach, who was considerably younger and less experienced than the other hard-headed advisers.

The naïve lay proposal was not being met with much enthusiasm. The clergy did not seem keen. You might say they were passively hostile, perhaps, like paid-up union men fearing they might be losing some of their hard-earned industrial conditions. They didn't want any layman looking over their shoulders into their affairs, giving advice and examining the books. During the discussions, Father Michael had been keeping his head down, saying as little as possible. Eventually the bishop had had enough. Too much talk. Important work to be done. Half-glancing at my mate, and before closing the meeting, he said,

'And do you want to say anything, Father?'

Addressing his clergy by their formal titles rather than their Christian names ensured an appropriate distance between the boss and his staff. Give any servant an inch and he'll challenge your authority.

Michael didn't know what to say. As a student he had eagerly supported any program that involved the laity, but that message was not popular in this setting. He had read the signs. Michael was not stupid. He bit his lip and said, 'I don't really know that I can contribute much – except, perhaps, to say that we should try to discern what Jesus might have done – what he would want.'

'Don't be silly, Father,' Bishop Tom retorted. 'How would anyone ever know?'

You can be sure that no one in the meeting-room, from the bishop down to the junior cleric, realised the full extent of what had just transpired. There, in the unprepossessing bishop's house in a steel city south of Sydney, a group of clerics in a tiny diocese at the end of the earth, far from Rome, was making a decision about what should guide the pastoral policy of the diocese. How did they decide what to do? What was essential, what important, what trivial and not worth the time and energy to discuss? What direction to take? What were the normative principles at the heart of any Christian community? At this distance in time and at the other end of the world, how important was Jesus and his message? And how could you ever know what his message was?

With his gruff remark, the bishop had summed up in a typical one-liner the principal problem confronting modern theological research – is Jesus our guide, and if so, how can we know what he intended? Where can we go to find out? The bishop, of all people, was surprisingly doubtful that he had the wherewithal to come to any practical conclusion. Funny for a gruff, old bishop, in an off-the-cuff remark, to cast a blanket of doubt on the whole foundation of Christian theology and spirituality. He couldn't even see the point of pausing for a moment to find out. Why waste valuable time?

Inadequate they might be, but we do have documentary sources from the Early Church archives that we can read and interpret, which might help find an answer to a question so central to the Christian faith.

Before we begin our main task – to track the place women occupied in his life – we should pause to identify places where we can learn something about Jesus, and then to paint a picture of this thirty-odd-year-old man who attracted such attention in his lifetime and generated such passionate reactions. Who was he? What was he like? Where did he come from? Why so controversial? Admirers on one side, powerful establishment opponents on the other and many in between, standing around, gawking, coming and going. What did he think? What was he trying to do?

CHAPTER THREE

Prospecting in a Paddock of Theology

Unfortunately we are not blessed with a video recording of events involving Jesus and his followers. Nothing on YouTube. No tape recording of him telling one of his parables or delivering his Sermon on the Mount where he is supposed to have announced those beautiful Beatitudes. No essay or poem has come to us written in his scratchy hand, or a letter he wrote home to his mother or to one of his friends in Nazareth. We don't know what he looked like – his size and weight, the colour of his hair or the cut of his jib. No medical records. Not even a hair of his head, or a sandal he wore, a book he had read, or one of his dusty robes. No statue or bust of the man. No painting. (Forget about The Shroud – no one can establish its provenance with even a sliver of probability.) Only memories of others, recorded forty or fifty years later. Not the memories of his mother, or of his father Joseph, or of his brothers and sisters – but the memories gathered by different communities and published under the name of at least one apostle, Matthew, and perhaps another, maybe John the son of Zebedee, but probably not, and under the names of two other men who had impeccable links to the early Christian communities – Mark and Luke.

On the available evidence there can be no serious dispute that Jesus existed – he walked the earth at the beginning of the first century, breathing the air of Palestine, and ended his life stretched out on a cross just outside Jerusalem. A real live person.

There are a few early references to him among contemporary pagan writers: in Suetonius' collection on the lives of the Roman Emperors, *De Vita Caesarum*, which he wrote in 121 AD; in the works of the Jewish historian Flavius Josephus, who was writing towards the end of the first century; and in *The Annals* of Tacitus, a Roman historian, who was also writing in the first few decades of the second century, around 120 AD. However, the details these three authors recorded about Jesus are sparse. A few scattered facts about his life and the trouble he had caused, but nothing to cast light on his personality or his preaching, and of course a total blackout on his attitude towards women. I should add that Gaius Suetonius Tranquillus had been a close friend of Pliny the Younger and that he might have been on Pliny's staff in the years 110-112 AD, while Pliny was serving as a governor in Asia Minor. In a letter to Emperor Trajan, Pliny had things to say about the Christians in Bithynia and the trouble they were causing there. From the start Christians were considered troublemakers, like the man after whom they were called.

The Bishop of Wollongong would have found out nothing from these few sources about what Jesus was thinking, about his attitude towards lay advisory councils, towards women or anything else. To answer his theological question 'How would we ever know?' he would have had to look elsewhere.

What more need I tell you other than we will be looking long and hard at the four Gospels, peering into their texts, searching under the surface and strolling round in the world in which they were compiled? But perhaps I should tell you a little more before I invite you to dive into the sparkling clear waters of the gospels.

However contaminated by prejudices or beliefs these waters are, our most reliable information comes almost exclusively from the theological portraits of Jesus designed by four anonymous writers or four teams of writers, and ascribed to Mark, Matthew, Luke and John. The four gospels are biased material like any primary documents (and more so), heavy with theology, loaded with metaphorical and awkward typological material, much of which has lost its power to fascinate a twenty-first century reader. Four extraordinary pieces of literature replete with stories told and re-told by faithful followers, to be read to members of a faith-community.

While the historian's task is to find a path through the tangle of what some would regard as blatant propaganda, each portrait projects a particular image of a real, historical person. Each evangelist, to a greater or lesser extent, painted a picture of a man who was socially and religiously on the fringe – an opponent of the religious elite and a champion of the poor and outcasts, of publicans and sinners, of foreigners and the unwashed. Each evangelist presents us with an image of a public figure who insisted on challenging those in authority, calling them to account, undermining their power base and encouraging his followers to treat laws and regulations with insouciance – a radical, counter-cultural, subversive personality who became an unpopular presence in the capital city and was put to death. In view of their early appearance on the scene, we can be reasonably confident that all four portrait painters, each in his own way, with his own insights and prejudices, his colours and brushstrokes, produced a recognisable image of the man in question, just as he was, living and breathing, moving about, preaching and causing trouble.

The first documents to appear and be preserved within the Christian tradition were written by the Apostle Paul who died, as far as we can tell, in Rome about 67 AD, before any of the four gospels had been composed. He had begun to write letters to his local communities in about the middle to late 50s. Probably at about the same time, a collection of Jesus' sayings was being put together (referred by scholars as the 'Q' source), and local Christian communities were making a brief recording of their memories of different events involving Jesus and his friends. Paul wrote his first letter to the Thessalonians (and probably not the second), a letter to his people in Galatia, two letters to the church in Corinth that are still to hand, a letter to the Philippians, another to the Romans and a brief note to his friend Philemon. Other letters, which were attributed, probably falsely, to Paul, began to appear on the scene sometime later. The author or authors of the second epistle to the Thessalonians and the epistle to the Colossians and the one to the Ephesians probably had had some close links to Paul. The pastoral epistles to Timothy and Titus are another story.

The gospel documents were written at different times, for readers of different communities, addressing different problems, but all four probably appeared within the latter half of the first century, though the finished version of John's Gospel may not have made an appearance until sometime in the early second century.

On the evidence of Papias of Hierapolis, who was writing in the early second century and was quoted by Eusebius in his *Historia Ecclesiastica* (3. 39. 15), Peter's interpreter (a man called Mark – probably the Mark referred to in 1 Peter 5:12) was the author of what is probably the earliest of the three Synoptic Gospels. It was undoubtedly preceded by the 'Q' source.

The evidence is thin but scholars have suggested Mark's work was written in Rome, soon after Peter's death, sometime between the late 60s and mid-70s; that is, approximately 30 or 40 odd years after Jesus' death and perhaps ten or so years after Paul's first letter to Corinth.

The Gospel of Matthew followed Mark's. While no one can now be sure, it probably preceded Luke's and appeared around the early to mid-80s.

An accurate dating of these four gospels is not necessary for the study we are to embark on here. However interesting the question might be, approximations can suffice. Luke's Gospel, the third of the Synoptics, became available about the same time as Matthew's, maybe a little later (though no one can say with any certainty) and most scholars say before the Gospel of John. But again, no one can say with any confidence. Sometime later, the author of Luke's Gospel appears to have written the story of the foundation of the early Christian communities and the spread of Jesus' message – The Acts of the Apostles. At about the same time, an anonymous author wrote a number of letters that he pretended Paul of Tarsus had dictated – two letters to a young bishop called Timothy and another to Titus – the Pastoral Epistles. The New Testament was taking shape.

Despite the repetition of an oral tradition capturing community memories of Jesus, and despite the gradual appearance of some primitive written records (some of which were almost certainly available to Mark, and later to the authors of the Gospels of Matthew and of Luke), we have to face the real possibility that during those critical thirty or forty years accurate memories would have faded. As a general rule, precise dates and details of events do not cross the barrier of decades without some variation and embellishment. Memory, even community-based memory, is often corrupted by rumours and false memories. Sitting in court day after day, judges know that despite the best will in the world, witnesses of the same event don't often agree on the conversation they had heard or the events they had seen.

By the time the gospels saw the light of day, the person of Jesus and the events surrounding his life, especially the pivotal events, had already been subjected to a good deal of discussion. From the earliest times, theological considerations had begun to be overlaid on the basic facts. His death had become a sacrifice. Using Old Testament points of reference, Christians had begun to view Jesus as the Paschal victim, a scapegoat, the promised Messiah, the suffering servant of Isaiah, a Moses figure, a Second Adam, the founder of a new dispensation, of a new order. The memories of events surrounding Jesus were soaking in a vat of theological considerations as the early community strove to extract meaning from his life and gruesome death, and to impose purpose on what had occurred over thirty years previously – or in the case of John's Gospel even longer – sixty or seventy years before. The early Christian historical lenses were tinted with theological shades and colours. The gospel composers were dependent on what was known at the time, what had been remembered, what had been recorded, what had been available.

The material included in each of the gospels was arranged in simple, often artificial, sequences. The authors positioned their account of incidents where they seemed best suited from a compositional or theological point of view. While the authors of Mark, Matthew and Luke, for example, positioned the wild Temple cleansing scene just before their Passion narratives, the author of John's Gospel set it at the beginning of Jesus' ministry. But these authors were not writing history as historians do today. The selection of their material, its place in the overall structure of the work, and the orientation given to a particular discrete passage were determined by the author's literary ability, his theological outlook and his purpose in response to the needs of his readership. None of the Synoptics, and more particularly, the Gospel of John, would pretend to be a literal and historically accurate account of events. The gospels were simply not that type of literature.

The author of John's Gospel (whoever he was) came to many of the events surrounding Jesus' life from a perspective, a tradition, that was completely different from the other three composers. You have only to run your eyes over the material to know that this gospel is a stand-out – much more theological; more complex and masterful, more mysterious, more multi-layered, more encrusted with religious symbols. In this document the author (or authors) developed imaginary and lengthy symbolic discourses, which they placed on the lips of Jesus. Though some scholars are now of the mind that John's Gospel may be more historically accurate than formerly thought, the greater distance between the author (or authors) and the events of Jesus' life made that gospel even more reliant than the other three on fallible memories and records.

None of the four gospels (and for that matter none of the other New Testament documents) provides an anthropological or theological treatise on women in the contemporary society or in the Christian community. None of the authors deliberately set out to deal with Jesus' attitude to women, or to describe in any detail their place within the life and ministry of the early communities. As in many other theological or ethical questions that demand our attention (and the attention of our bishops), we have to read between the lines. We have to read carefully the narratives of particular events or the records dealing with particular pastoral problems. We need to look behind the text, explore the presuppositions, examine the immediate as well as the general cultural contexts, comparing and contrasting, extracting general principles and buried attitudes in order to develop some coherent picture of how Jesus treated the women with whom he came into daily contact. We need to observe how they treated him, and later, how these women fitted into the early Christian communities, what their place was, and how they were involved in ministry within the early setting.

Originally, a particular author or group of contributors put together a composite text from a variety of sources, gathering material to address a number of current problems. They assembled their material according to a particular plan, to address a particular purpose, to be read or heard by a particular group of readers or listeners. The four gospels, The Acts of the Apostles and the Pauline letters and the other letters in the library we call the New Testament all fit this profile. Each document came out of a particular cultural setting, was put together by an individual author or composer and was made available mostly in a community gathering.

Later, the very same document became available to a larger audience, to people in different places. Gradually it became associated with other similar documents written or assembled by other composers, with material from similar and different sources, to be accepted, read and reflected on by believers from other cultures. Readers from other times and other cultures were invited to search for meaning in these documents and to find nourishment there. A few centuries later, a number of these same documents were assembled into a collection and gradually the canon or an authorised collection was established: a complicated story of compilation, preservation, translations and reception over many centuries.

In the 21st century, this collection of writings – including our four gospels, various letters, histories and poetic dream-literature, after being read, analysed and discussed from one century to the next in Europe, Egypt, North Africa, the Americas – has become available to us, to be read and reflected on in Australia, in a profoundly different cultural setting. Be warned! This rich evolutionary story must be borne in mind when we come to read and interpret passages in the gospels or in the epistles of Paul.

To begin with, I want to explore how the composers of our gospels sought to depict Jesus to their readers, to the new and undoubtedly fascinated members of the early Christian communities, forty, fifty, sixty years after the Preacher's death and disappearance. What did they personally remember (if anything) about this strange person who had lived among them? And what memories of him had been told and retold – memories that they wanted to capture and preserve and, yes, embellish? What aspects of his life did they recall and seek to highlight? The sayings were remembered, repeated, recorded and preserved for the believers when they gathered to share, to pray and sing together, and to celebrate. How did these authors interpret this man's life and death? What spin did they intend to put on his actions, on his words? And more particularly from my point of view, how did they remember their Teacher engaging with the women around him – speaking to them, sharing their food and their ideas, embracing them, involving them in his ministry?

Our gospels were composed for the early Christian communities of the first century. Then they were copied and handed on, and handed down to the next generation, and on and on, one generation after another, each reading the stories, reflecting on the content, interpreting the message, discovering, exploring, and emphasising different sayings, different events, using the text to search for answers to new problems. These precious works were woven into the fabric of society down the centuries, into the evolving cultures of Europe and the Middle East, inspiring works of art, theological discussion and debates, political views, poems, legends, and, from time to time, causing wars.

Fascinating as the whole story is, I am interested in the portrait of Jesus as it was developed in the first century for the early Christians. Scholars have studied ancient manuscripts, prepared and revised critical versions of the texts, and translated them into various languages. These translations were authenticated, printed and distributed to the general public. Institutions invite us to read and study them, search them carefully for meaning, reflect on them and find in them a guide for our lives. Believers accept these four books as the official principal source material from which we are encouraged to produce an image of Jesus. They are the primeval source of all that the Christian churches teach. They enjoy a pre-eminent status within the institution – at least in principle, if not in fact.

This study is not just an historical exercise, however interesting an exercise that might be. Our gospels (and the other New

Testament documents) operate in today's world. They have been read by millions and millions of people before us. But we read them now. They belong to us. They come to us in our language and we filter them through our needs, our problems, our lives, our insights and prejudices.

You might think that these writings are all the same – just one collection of different texts. All of the same value – one letter the same as another – no difference between the first letter to the Thessalonians and Paul's epistle to the Romans; one of the gospels on a par with The Apocalypse. I don't agree. As far as I'm concerned, our four gospels are more important, more central, and because they re-create Jesus for us – recording his parables and sayings – they should be more central and powerful in determining Christian standards and norms within our churches than any of the other documents which make up the New Testament.

I believe the foundation of the religious institutions that make Christ visible in the world, the source of their impetus and their mission, must be found primarily in these four canonical gospels. The institution ignores this material at its peril. Its integrity and authenticity depend on them, and each generation of Christians is challenged to approach this source material with fresh eyes, reading it as though for the first time, discovering a message about life and death, about mankind and the world that will resonate loudly, persuasively, beautifully in the contemporary world.

But before we enter the territory which is the focus of this study, namely, women in the life and mission of Jesus as described by the four writers of the Early Church, we must explore the fertile landscape cultivated by these evangelists – Jesus as a person. We must then examine the heart of the message Jesus preached, and before training our gaze on the women in Jesus' life, we should attempt to gain some idea as to what it was like to be a woman in a man's world in Palestine in the first century.

CHAPTER FOUR

A First Century Portrait of a Preacher

The Jesus of the Gospels comes across as the archetypal stranger, the classical outsider and troublemaker; a tough critic of the Jewish establishment, an uncompromising opponent of religion in its institutional uniform – a man given to dismissing the importance of the law in all its superficial, trivial manifestations. People rather than regulations. Interior realities rather than external formalities. Against religion and its institutions, its man-made rules and dogmas. Against wealth and power. Distant, aloof, unsettling. A loner who was completely indifferent to what others thought of him or expected from him. A presence that dominated the scene wherever he went. Surrounded by a mysterious power, an inexplicable wisdom and gushing with an interior authority.

Jesus appeared on the public stage at the age of about thirty, born and bred in the mountains of Judea, with the broad uncultured accent of a mountain man from the north. He had come out of nowhere, unemployed and with no friends or companions save for one – a crazy man called John the Baptiser. A solitary figure, uprooted from family and home, often found wandering alone in deserted, mountainous areas, who had come to town to teach and cause trouble. A visionary. A prophet. Dreaming dreams, revealing secrets, uncovering the mystery hidden at the heart of reality.

At the time, Nazareth was a Jewish settlement nestled in the hill country of Lower Galilee – a village so obscure that it didn't rate a mention in the literature of the Old Testament, or by Josephus, or Philo, or in the early rabbinic writings, or in the pseudo-epigraphic books. Completely shrouded in an anonymous silence. A village of maybe forty or fifty local families, mainly farming folk, artisans like Joseph's crowd, and traders – practically all of whom were Jews. The little synagogue in which Jesus was later to preach might have supported a basic educational program for young boys like Jesus, with a teacher attached. The local sacristan might have been multi-skilled and engaged to double in the role.

The capital of Galilee, Sepphoris, largely inhabited by foreigners and Gentiles, a lively centre of trade, was a two-hour journey on foot to the north. Jesus' home-town was isolated in the hills, hidden among market gardens, orchards, vineyards and olive groves, in a peaceful rural setting.

Judaism as practised by the locals would have been a strongly conservative version of the Jewish faith. The men and their women would have tended to be hostile and suspicious of the Pharisaic niceties on offer in the south. As Galilean peasants, their lives and faith were solidly grounded in the Mosaic Law, in the Temple and its rituals far away in Jerusalem, the practice of circumcision and the ceremonies conducted in the local synagogue – the reading of the sacred texts, preaching and the rhythmic recitation of the psalms. These men and their women were not attracted to the novelties and subtleties of the elite Pharisaical classes. Basic, practical, farming, God-fearing people.

No-one has a clear idea of what formal education Jesus had received, or even where he had spent the twenty or so years after his brief taste of youthful independence in Jerusalem. His life before he hit the rough road to Jerusalem is a closed book. No one thought to write a biography to dress this electric figure in the details of a mundane life. The author of Luke's Gospel would have us believe that at an early age (the same age as I had attained when I went away to the seminary to become one of his priests), a consciousness of his special divine vocation was dawning in Jesus' brain. As the story goes, his first recorded words were addressed to his parents and come in the form of what appears to have been an important question, perhaps even a little put-down: 'Did you not know that I must look to my Father's affairs?'

Or, as another translator reads the Greek text: 'Did you not know that I must be in my Father's house?' Whatever the translation, according to the Gospel of Luke this young man was claiming that he saw himself as being called to special duties and, in order to fulfil his Father's wishes, he needed to be out and about, in discussion with the Temple theologians and lawyers, alone and free, even from parental supervision.

What an extraordinary and puzzling interchange between a young man of twelve and his pious parents! Luke's author seems to have wanted his readers to accept that Jesus had been special from an early age – a boy with great promise, on a mission from beyond. Apart from this curious incident, however, we know nothing of what Jesus' life was like before he burst onto the scene at the age of about thirty; nothing of his schooling, apprenticeship, overseas trips, holidays, sporting interests, girlfriends – nothing. A blank canvas.

At the age of twelve, Jesus had been found in the Temple area, sitting among the teachers, listening to them and asking questions. All who heard him were amazed at his understanding and his answers. The author was telling his readers that he had heard reports that from an early age Jesus had been at home among the teachers in Jerusalem and that they were in awe of him. He was comfortable in their classroom, taking notice and ready to learn. The depth of his knowledge and understanding was remarkable. At twelve, he could hold his own in the company of city teachers of the Law and the Prophets. As far as the early Christian community was concerned (though it seems something like the beginning of a Jesus legend), as a pre-teenager, Jesus was well advanced in his religious education. If the story is half true, we can presume with some confidence that he had attended school in Nazareth, that he had been introduced to the dreaming of his people and that he had perhaps learnt to read some passages of the sacred books.

For a number of reasons, we can probably conclude that Jesus' religious formation, in his family and most likely in the boys school attached to the synagogue, was intense and profound, and that it included reading and discussing passages in Hebrew of Palestine's sacred literature. As a thirty-year-old, his disciples and listeners regarded him as a rabbi, as a teacher who spoke with surprising authority. The gospel writers tell stories of his preaching in the synagogues. In his adult life, his mind was fiercely focused on the Jewish faith and its practices. The gospel authors reported on his energetic participation in learned disputes on religious subjects with students of the Law, with the intellectuals from the city, the priests and Pharisees. As we see him in the literature, he was able to hold his own in elite company and win an argument. His ability in legal and religious debates with pious Pharisees, with scribes and the intelligentsia of Jerusalem would tend to suggest that he could read and understand his people's sacred literature.

The author of John's Gospel tells the story that in the middle of the Feast of Tabernacles, Jesus had gone up to the Temple 'and taught' there. His Jewish listeners were astonished to hear him. He had made a big impression. They couldn't understand how Jesus had come by his level of sophistication. His very presence engendered awe – or hostility:

> How is it that this stranger from Nazareth is able to display such wisdom and knowledge? Where did he learn to conduct a theological discussion based on our sacred books? He hasn't studied under any of our established rabbis or graduated from one of our schools of learning. The power of his words is remarkable. He is able to demand attention and fascinate the crowds.*

The image of Jesus that the Gospel writers sought to project was of a person who was passionate about religious practices, well-versed in the sacred literature of his people, a gifted preacher and teacher with an uncommon ability to engage the establishment in debate and confront important issues, undoubtedly able to read the Hebrew literature which was later to become the Bible – a man who conversed in Aramaic but could read Hebrew. It is doubtful, however, whether he could write, and if so, to what extent. In his day, writing was generally restricted to the upper levels of the bureaucracy and not necessarily allied to the skill of reading, as it is today.

The author of Luke recounted an expanded version of the story that had been told by the authors of Mark and Matthew (Luke 4:16-30). Jesus was in Nazareth 'where he had been brought up' and as was customary, he went to the synagogue on the Sabbath as any practising Jewish man would have done. According to the story, he read to the community – so he had learnt to read. But who had taught him? His mother? Maybe, if she herself had been able to read – and we have no idea whether she could or not. In those days, especially in the rural north, girls were not usually enrolled in any formal education program. So, if not Mary, then who? Joseph? A local rabbi? A scribe attached to the synagogue in the village? The local sacristan?

The synagogue people had listened with open mouths and wondered at his gracious words. After all, they all knew him. They knew where he had come from. He was only the son of Joseph the carpenter – and they knew his father too. In the course of the exchange, Jesus chided and riled them. They had thought he was just a pretty ordinary nobody, so he set out to teach them a lesson.

According to the Jewish tradition, God was unpredictable. His ways were mysterious. He preferred nobodies and did the unexpected. Rather than one of the many worthy poverty-stricken widows of Palestine he could have helped, God had preferred someone from the land of Sidon, the widow of Zarephath. And ignoring the many deserving lepers in Palestine, God had chosen to heal Naaman the Syrian. So Jesus' lesson to his own villagers was – don't be deceived. Don't presume. Don't think you can anticipate what God will do. Don't assume you can control the time or the place where God will appear. You're in for a big surprise. I've got news for you.

> You might think that I am just a nobody. And I am. But, like in the past, God has taken me in hand. Like it or not, I am his chosen one, his prophet, the anointed one. I will speak to you of dreams and visions that come above.*

Again, if the story is true, the villagers were outraged. So full of anger that Jesus was forced to escape before they did him harm. He was electrified and sparks were flying. A nobody who could frighten people and generate hostility.

In brief, the image that the gospels depict of Jesus is of a man who could read and teach, one who could find a passage in the manuscript containing the words of the prophet Isaiah, who knew of the prophets Elijah and Elisha and of the contents of the narrative in 1 Kings 17 and 2 Kings 5. He was not the ignorant nobody they presumed him to be. He was a gifted teacher.

But he was only a layman, in a highly structured religious culture – not a trained, professional lawyer, or a scribe, or a priest, or a registered member of any of the exclusive Jewish schools. He came from a pious Jewish family. According to the story, he appeared on the scene in Galilee, out of the desert: a deeply religious man, a visionary, a preacher with a message about a mysterious kingdom, about a spiritual experience open to all, with an original message about the role of law in ordinary people's lives – a new law of love and freedom, a law engraved on their hearts. He encapsulated his fascinating message in juicy tidbits – in parables and pithy epigrams. A powerful storyteller, a remarkable teacher, an uncomfortable prophetic figure and wonder-worker with mysterious, personal powers over demons and illnesses, even over death – at least that's how the gospel writers depict this mysterious figure.

He was not a philosopher or a theologian, but after his execution he became the focus of a controversial theological vision with profoundly personal and cosmological dimensions. As the members of the Christian communities began to reflect on the meaning of this man's short, turbulent life and on the significance of his presence among them, it gradually dawned on them that he was the Messiah who had been anticipated by the Jewish prophets. He became the long-awaited redeemer, a sacrificial victim, a scapegoat, an eternal high priest, a second Adam, a new Moses, the mythological Son of Man from the Book of Daniel, the Suffering Servant of Isaiah, the first-born of all creation, the revelation of the Father, the fulfilment of the divine plan for mankind and the world, above powers of heaven, above the choirs of angels and archangels. And centuries later, a handsome man in priestly vestments, wearing a royal crown, hanging triumphantly on a cross, the second person of a divine Trinity, Christ the King. And more recently, the melancholic bearded man with doe eyes pointing to his wounded Sacred Heart and complaining of being misunderstood.

Behind these later theological constructs and in their shadow stood a real person who had to eat and sleep, who had lived with his mother and father in a mountain village. He had wandered around Palestine, along highways and byways, in and out of towns and villages. He had mixed and mingled, enjoying life, sharing his vision of the world. He had breathed the air of his homeland, smelt the perfumes and the odours of the streets, observed the birds high in the sky, listened to crickets in the fields and arguments in the synagogues and felt the hot desert wind on his face. As he hung on the cross, accused of blasphemy and sedition, mushy fluids, blood mixed with sweat and urine, oozed and dripped from his tortured body. The memory of a real, flesh-and-blood person is hidden behind the many theological and metaphorical interpretations which followed his death and have dribbled out of busy pens over many centuries.

In fact, as we see him portrayed in our four gospels, (though not in the writings of Paul, The Acts of the Apostles or the other New Testament literature) Jesus was a mysterious and rebellious figure from 'out of town', who fulminated against the established religious institutions, against petty regulations, pomp and privilege, against the thick civil servants and brainless bureaucrats of his time. As the story unwinds, Jesus was seen surrounded by bullies and religious thugs from Jerusalem. The gospel composers recorded the outpourings of vitriol he directed at the men (always men) who were in power – hypocrites, cold, pale marble sepulchers, wind-bags, window-dressers, humbugs, charlatans full of pious cant, sanctimonious snakes in the grass. Apparently, as they remembered it, Jesus hadn't held his fire.

Sometimes Jesus comes to us as a homeless vagrant, a lone figure praying in the mountains, a guru with an untidy band of followers, with fishermen and a tax collector in tow. At other times we see him as a charismatic figure from the north, with a team of disciples, come to the city to stir up trouble, to clear God's Temple of avaricious money-changers and to disrupt the business model of the Temple priests. He was intent on delivering his uncomfortable message, mocking and scarifying the pompous charlatans in power. He wanted to educate and enlighten, to reveal the secrets of an alternative world and to fulfil the promise that God had made to Palestine. His mission was to conclude a new covenant between God and his people and to elevate the Mosaic Law to an interior regime of love and freedom written on the hearts of true believers. As the gospel authors would have it, this was the stranger whom the men and women of Palestine encountered every day, over a period of three years, more or less.

There is little indication in any of the gospels about where Jesus and his crew got their money to survive day by day. There was often a crowd of them: apostles, disciples, occasional followers and hangers-on, sometimes in isolated dark spots, far from shops and produce markets. Judas had been put in charge of the kitty; the communal pocket money probably came from a few rich women who were following Jesus around, from the occasional handout, from faceless supporters. Joseph of Arimathea and the little man who had climbed into the sycamore tree were probably both rich enough to have made a decent contribution.

But Jesus' life with his disciples seems to have been a tenuous existence. A meal here and there, sometimes with the elite, often with the outcasts. A bed in the corner. A nap under a tree, in a field, by the side of the road. Throughout it all, Jesus maintained his dignity. He was his own man, indebted to no one, in touch with himself and touched with a mysterious presence from on high. If he had learnt a trade from his father, there is no suggestion in any of the early literature that Jesus had hammered a nail or driven a screw to support himself or his team. The Apostle Paul was used to earning his keep by practising his trade as a tent-maker as he journeyed from town to town. Jesus had adopted a different policy. He believed that any labourer (and a preacher of the good news was a labourer) deserved his wages and should be looked after by those he was serving.

The elite in Jerusalem, the bureaucrats, the learned and the Pharisees, had kept him under surveillance and had concluded that he was a danger to peace and good order – and to them. They spun the message that he was able to perform wonders because he was possessed by the prince of demons. But once they had given voice to their theological slur in the presence of the assembled crowd, Jesus had engaged them in debate and had crushed them with his logic and his ridicule. He referred to them as 'a brood of vipers', and mocked them with his razor-sharp wit: 'How can anyone believe what you say when you speak such nonsense?'*

He told his listeners that unless their own righteousness exceeded that of their religious leaders, they had no chance of finding their way into the Kingdom of Heaven:

> When you give alms, sound no trumpet before you, as the hypocrites do in the synagogues and in the streets, that they may be praised by men. I tell you, they have their reward … When you pray, don't copy the hypocrites among you. They love to stand and pray in the synagogues and at the street corners. They love to be seen. I tell you, they have their reward. When you fast, don't look sad or shaggy like the hypocrites among us do. They disfigure their faces that they might be seen fasting. I'll tell you again, they have their reward. (Matt 6:2, 5 and 16)*

When it came to letting his followers and the crowds know what he thought of the Jewish establishment, Jesus did not speak out of the side of his mouth. No soft, weasel words. No spin. He was not a politician working the crowd, looking for votes.

> The scribes and the Pharisees preach, but don't practise. They package up heavy burdens which are hard to bear, and they lay them on men's shoulders, but they themselves refuse to move them with their finger. They do everything to be seen by men. They make their phylacteries broad and their fringes long, and they love the place of honour at feasts and the best seats in the synagogues, and salutations in the marketplace, and being called Rabbi. (Matt 23:ff)*

He nailed them. Hypocrites. Blind guides and sightless fools. White-washed tombs. Serpents and vipers. According to the gospels, Jesus was punching well above his weight – and making enemies. He had spoken out against the religious leaders of his day – their arrogance, their hypocrisy, their wish to occupy the first places at public functions, their exploitation of the poor, their love of empty titles, of bells and whistles, useless badges, drums and silly insignias. For most of his life, as the story is told, he was either under attack himself, or confronting those in authority – getting under their skin, undermining their authority and inviting his followers to see the established elite as they were, without their clothes and titles. The four official gospels bear witness to this Jesus.

Considering that Jesus had been a good Jewish boy, educated in the law and familiar with his Jewish sacred literature, as a young adult he was to demonstrate a shocking disregard, at least according to the gospels, for the Mosaic Law and for the customs of his religion. Contrary to the law, he had eaten with publicans and sinners. He had not observed the ritual requirements of fasting, or of washing hands before eating, and he had not required his followers to obey these ritual prohibitions. He had ignored the petty laws forbidding even the smallest job to be done on the Sabbath – and he had turned his back and shrugged his shoulders when his followers ignored these petty rules. He had not concerned himself with trivia and nonsense.

Jesus' brazen behaviour had not gone unnoticed. In public, and defying all convention, he had healed a paralytic on the Sabbath; he had cured a man with a withered hand – on the Sabbath; and he had allowed his hungry band of followers to pluck ears of grain and eat them – again on the Sabbath. Jesus had not discreetly bent the regulations or quietly flouted the law policed by the authorities. He had argued his case, challenged his opponents' world-view, and reinterpreted the very foundation of their laws and their understanding of accepted religious practices. He had subjected the establishment's religious system to a radical re-examination, and if he was right, their precious world should have been in a state of collapse. Their authority, their power base, their position and their privileges had been questioned by this preacher from the hills. Jesus had not been one of them. He had not attended their schools or their institutions of higher learning. He wasn't a member of their club. He had been telling his many listeners that those in authority were dumb and wrong, leading people astray – away from God. It was obvious he had to be stopped.

When he had finally arrived in Jerusalem, found accommodation and began to explore his surroundings, Jesus grew more and more distressed. He had found the city to be a cold, inhospitable, even hostile place. An unholy city occupied by zealous, moralistic clerics, self-satisfied and rather pompous intellectuals, greedy financiers, shady go-getters, squabbling religious sects and a fickle, noisy mob. Jesus wept over the city of David, like a grieving mother forced to stand and watch her child destroy himself. He was a figure charged with the full gamut of human emotion – anger, sadness, empathy, compassion, love and loneliness.

Caiaphas was the most influential official in Jerusalem. For eighteen years, he had enjoyed being the high priest, with all the perks that went with the office. He held control over the 71-man Sanhedrin (not one woman on the board of governors!) the supreme council charged with policing the civil and religious law. And he had made a point of establishing strong bonds with the occupying Roman forces.

Jesus was a threat to Caiaphas's position and authority, and he was making trouble for Rome. A danger to society. A threat to the annual income of the Temple priests. They had had a good business going, involving an impressive revenue stream. God's little people had to pay the Temple officials for ritual bathing in the precincts of Solomon's Temple, to purify themselves before offering a sacrifice or engaging in an act of worship. A Jewish man could not even approach the Temple until he was ritually pure –

and the priests held a commercial monopoly on the process. This was a thriving business: people paid for baths, for birds and animals to sacrifice, dropping money-offerings in the boxes strategically placed throughout the Temple precincts, and paying a percentage to the moneychangers. The bottom line on the balance sheets was always in the black.

Jesus had been teaching that the elaborate purity rituals that the priests and scribes had developed were a religious con. The whole religious program was nonsense. As the prophets had all said before him, God was interested in justice and fairness, in the care of his poor and dispossessed. As far as he was concerned, religious practice had developed into an elaborate hoax. He was familiar with his Jewish sacred literature in ways that those in authority had forgotten:

> What I desire is steadfast love and not sacrifice; the knowledge of God rather than any burnt offering. (Hosea 6:6)

> What does God require of you? To act with justice, to love kindness and to walk humbly with your God. (Micah 6:8)

His preaching had become bad news for the whole Temple program. When he had driven the bankers from the Temple and overthrown their money stalls, accusing them of turning his Father's house into a den of thieves, Caiaphas decided Jesus had to go. It was best for all – priests, financiers, accountants, traders, lawyers, Romans. A good, practical decision.

All four gospels record the incident of Jesus cleansing the Temple. The four authors wanted their readers to know this particular explosive dimension of Jesus' personality: righteous anger and in-your-face confrontation. The author of Mark was the first to record the story:

> And they came to Jerusalem. And he entered the Temple and began to drive out those who sold and those who bought in the

> Temple, and he overturned the tables of the moneychangers and the seats of those who sold pigeons; and he would not allow anyone to carry anything through the Temple. And he taught, and said to them, "is it not written, "my house shall be called house of prayer for all the nations"? But you have made it a den of robbers." And the chief priests and the scribes heard it and sought a way to destroy him; for they feared him, because so many good people were astonished at his teaching. (Mark 11:15-18)

Imagine the reaction of the Jewish clergy and their business-partners:

> 'What's this madman doing? Everything we've heard about him is true. Crazy. Ruining a good money-earner. Everything we've worked for all our lives. We know now why those bloody university graduates and Pharisees are so stirred up. There's no doubt in our mind that they're right. Let's get rid of him.'*

Though on examination the Roman governor had found no crime in him, Jesus was described in the Gospel of John as an evil-doer, a 'malefactor'. Luke reported that when Jesus came before Pilate on the first occasion, he had been accused of perverting the nation, stirring up the people, teaching up and down the country, from Galilee to Jerusalem, forbidding people to pay tribute to Caesar and claiming to be Christ the King. The second time, Luke tells us he was again accused of perverting the nation. When Jesus was dragged before the Jewish religious courts, he was accused of claiming to be the Christ and the Son of God, the son of the Blessed one, the Son of Man sitting at the right hand of the powers and coming on a cloud of heaven, and able to rebuild the great Temple in three days.

On finding him guilty of blasphemy, the Jewish judicial system determined he should be crucified. Then, when Jesus appeared before the Roman courts, under the awesome foreign jurisdiction of Governor Pilate, many charges were levelled against him by the chief priests, the elders and scribes. The one charge specified in the Gospel of John (a charge that never held water) was that he had claimed to be 'the King of the Jews' – an affront to the authority of Rome. An act of treason. The crime of rebellion. 'Anyone who makes himself a king sets himself against Caesar.'

In the end, those he had offended nailed Jesus to a cross, just outside the city of Jerusalem, with a brigand on his right and another on his left. Three together, crucified by the occupying Roman authorities under pressure from the Jewish elite. According to the story, he had been accused by Jewish officials, condemned by a series of religious kangaroo courts, and put to death by conspiring with foreign soldiers after the Roman governor had crumbled to establishment pressure and popular demand. But this was not the end of their troubles. There was more to come.

A powerful prophet. A visionary. A wonder-worker. A man of the people. An outsider. A deeply religious man of God, destined to end his life in tragedy and to inspire a worldwide revolution.

CHAPTER FIVE

The Backdrop to a Drama
Jesus' Message of a Kingdom

The way women are seen by others, the way they see themselves, the way they are treated in a society inevitably appears within a much wider context. Their place in any community is a function of some unspoken cultural ideology and an ensemble of features that control the daily life of everyone: whether the society is structured on a rigid patriarchal grid, the principles governing things like inheritance laws and marriage customs; who is recognised as being able to exercise power and make decisions; who enacts the laws, conducts the trials and imposes punishments. In any society women (and men), like the poor or the rich, like the old, the fit and the sick, fit into a broader worldview dominated by a conglomeration of beliefs and prejudices, of shared attitudes and values.

Palestine, at the time of Mary and Joseph and their son Jesus, was no different and we will soon make an effort to gain some idea as to where women stood in that society. However, in order to understand where Jesus was coming from regarding the place of men and women in his religious world, we have to take a step to the side in an attempt to reconstruct the religious mindset that determined how he viewed the world. We need to understand how he saw the structures of power and authority within his world, what he saw in the background when he looked at a woman, what he heard when a woman spoke to him, how he related to them, and how he welcomed their response to him and his mob.

The story is told in several of the gospels that the mother of John and James had requested Jesus to grant places of influence to her two boys, one on his right hand, the other on his left, in his kingdom. But their mother had misinterpreted all the signs. She had presumed that Jesus was going to take over the government of Palestine and set himself up with all the paraphernalia, machinery and impedimenta of 'good' government, and that her sons would naturally be an important part of the show.

She was not the only one to have missed the point. Even the apostles had let their imagination run riot, expecting Jesus to make his move on the levers of power and re-establish the empire of King David. Apparently, without the least encouragement, they had become quite delusional. But every son and daughter of Abraham had been waiting for the messiah to make his move, to take over the reins of power, expel the filthy Roman carpetbaggers and bask in the glow of Palestine's past glories.

It must have been a bitter blow to Mrs Zebedee, to Peter and the apostles as well as to all the other followers, to be told by Jesus that had no intention of staging any *coup d'état*. If they thought he had been talking about a kingdom in which he would be king, they were all in for a rude shock. He had other plans. He was not what they had thought him to be. Nothing remotely like a ruler. Not even a senior bureaucrat, a mandarin, a high priest or pope. He had no ambition to exercise authority, or any desire to allot positions in a kingdom, or to confer favours on his friends. He was destined to wash feet and to be racked to death on a cross. He had been functioning in a different world from that of the ambitious mother of James and John, and of his other apostles. In his world it was not given to him to appoint his friends to high office in any worldly kingdom.

Jesus appears in different guises in the gospel literature and the other early Christian writings – as the Messiah, as a redeemer, the sacrificial Lamb of God, a law-giver like Moses, a prophet, a preacher, a teacher, a wonder-worker, the Suffering Servant of Isaiah, a second Adam, as Elijah come back to earth. The convergence of these roles in the one individual would become extremely dense and complicated, as the history of theology demonstrates. But according to the gospel authors, the principal message Jesus preached focused on the simple image of a kingdom, whatever later theological interpretations were later laid over the message.

Jesus is depicted in the gospels as the prophet *par excellence* who was driven to proclaim the message of a kingdom. In some low-key way, this Elijah-like miracle-worker had arrived on the scene to make the Kingdom of God a present and palpable reality for his believing followers.

But he was not just a prophet. He was also a lay teacher who had the power to interpret the Law of Moses and to teach his people what laws were important and how to observe them. He possessed a mesmerising and personal authority. This teacher was not reliant, like all the others, on the worn-out traditions of the past. He was free to draw on his own powerful intuitions. Though there were other preachers and other wonder-workers plying their trade in Palestine, this mysterious, multidimensional figure (as depicted by the gospels) was a unique presence in the midst of the Jewish people in the early part of the first century.

The motif of 'the Kingdom of God' had made a minor appearance in the literature of the Old Testament. As a practising Jewish boy, Jesus would almost certainly have been aware of the image and, as an adult, he embraced it enthusiastically and made it the centrepiece of his religious message. Consequently, though it is surprisingly absent in the letters of the New Testament, the symbol appears in the Gospels in many different contexts, leavening a variety of literary forms – parables, prayers, beatitudes, eschatological prophesies, and the wonder stories (especially the exorcisms and healings). It is at the basis of the many statements attributed to Jesus that set out the prerequisites for entrance into the kingdom.

If we accept the say-so of the gospel authors, the symbol 'Kingdom of God' (and its equivalent 'Kingdom of Heaven') was right at the heart of Jesus' message: thirteen appearances in Mark's Gospel, thirteen estimated appearances in the now non-extant Q source, twenty-five in Matthew's and six in Luke's. There can be little doubt that this image was the molten lava bubbling to the surface of Jesus' message. It formed a major part (in fact, some would say, *the* major feature) of his teachings.

The institutions of our religious faith as we have come to know them – the Roman curia, the pope and his college of cardinals, the local parish, the diocesan bureaucracy, the St Vincent de Paul and Caritas Australia – belong to the here and now. But these institutions and organisations have roots (some of them quite tenuous roots) buried in the past. Our ecclesiastical organisations have come out of the shadows of the past to provide a building and social structures in which we can hear and receive Jesus' life-giving message, where we can pass it on to others in its compromised purity. Down below the surface of those features is the kingdom as preached by Jesus. This kingdom is in essence a future reality, a dream preserved within a small but powerful seed hidden in the ground, and each of us, each age, and each culture is only a microscopic part of a long unfolding process.

Jesus was someone who lived centuries ago in a foreign world, but the community memory of him renders him both significant and mysteriously present today, still preaching to us in order to propel us into the future, to contribute by our tiny acts of faith to the evolution of a kingdom of hope and glory. We water the seeds already planted by others, in the hope that these seeds hold future promises to be realised. By the power of their faith, Christians are builders of a future, not peddlers of a past, workers in a vineyard producing a crop yet to be harvested, prophets of a future which does not belong to us, daydreamers gazing hopefully into the distance, not weary sleepwalkers peering nostalgically in the disappearing shadows of the past.

Jesus preached a mysterious muddle of images to point the true listener – the attentive listener with ears keen to hear – in the direction of a kingdom, and to point the true searcher with sharp eyes to see the signs buried in the present. Time and again, according to the writers, Jesus returned to his central message and explained what he wanted his listeners to hear and understand, speaking in riddles, aphorisms and parables. No simple statement could encapsulate all that had to be said on the topic, but in order to provide a background to our study of women in the life of Jesus we must try to capture some of the principal elements of this message.

According to the author of the Gospel of Mark, early in his ministry Jesus had been sitting in a boat addressing a crowd that had gathered on the beach. He was teaching them in a way they could understand. While for those outside his circle his message was framed in parables, Jesus used to share the secret of the kingdom with some of his closer followers and explain his parables to them.

Mark has Jesus speaking to the crowd and to his disciples in riddles. He left them scratching their heads, wondering what on earth he was saying, or what the meaning of life was. For example, try to unravel this dense saying of the Preacher:

> The measure you give will be the measure you get, and still more will be given to you. For to him who has will more be given, and from him who has not, even what he has will be taken away. (Mark 4:24-25)

Jesus told his listeners that the Kingdom of God was like a man scattering seed on the ground. Without his knowledge and while he slept, the seeds grew – the delicate leaf piercing the earth, the ear swelling, the grain maturing. When the grain was ready and ripe, the farmer would come out and wield his sickle to harvest his crop. The kingdom was a process, but under God's mysterious direction.

Again, as Jesus was supposed to have said, the Kingdom of God was like a mustard seed which, according to the storyteller, was the smallest of all the seeds on earth, but when it germinated and grew, it became the greatest of all the shrubs, and the birds would make their nests in its shade. The lesson: the kingdom that Jesus was preaching was almost invisible among us – a speck in the ground, but with huge potential to become a haven for a multitude, a place for people seeking safe shelter and somewhere to feel at home. The kingdom might have appeared insignificant, but it had the makings of a future real estate to accommodate the masses. To live in the same zone as God, we have to be touched with the same divine madness. A home for a multitude where everyone would be welcome.

The author of Matthew's Gospel changed the scene and stationed Jesus on top of a mountain, like a second Moses on Mount Sinai. The author narrated the story of Jesus' formal declaration to his disciples and to a crowd of bystanders, setting out a charter for the kingdom. In the open-air gathering, we see Jesus inaugurating a new world, establishing a new way of living for his followers, and a different way of relating to God and to each other – fulfilling and transcending the expectations of those who had gone before him. A divine secret being revealed about a nation of saints, about a kingdom which was not founded on power, or wealth, or privilege, or nationalistic pride and the domination of others, but based on humble service, on the experience of love and forgiveness, on sharing and searching.

According to the author of Matthew's Gospel, Jesus began his charter for the new order by declaring that the poor in spirit were blessed because the Kingdom of Heaven belonged to them, and to those who were being persecuted in the cause of righteousness. One of the principal features of Jesus' vision was that in the Kingdom of Heaven priority status would be accorded to the poor, the oppressed and the marginalised. Consequently, Jesus' ministry to the poor and the outcast was to be front and centre. These people were especially loved and cherished by the God he knew and whom he met face-to-face in prayer.

According to Jesus, the Kingdom of Heaven demanded an indifference to possessions and a simple trust in the providence of the God who 'feeds the birds of the air and clothes the lilies of the fields'. A true believer had to first seek the Kingdom of God and his righteousness, because he couldn't serve two masters – God and Mammon. No divided loyalties.

Stories were Jesus' preferred mode of teaching. He told of a rich man who was clothed in purple and fine linen and who feasted 'sumptuously' every day – an arrogant monster who ignored the nondescript creature at his gate who was the one whom angels would transport to Abraham's bosom. And Jesus told the story of the rich farmer who was communicating so confidently with himself, advising his soul to relax, to sit back, to eat, drink and make merry, with plenty of grain in his enlarged silos – the farmer whom Jesus had described as a fool and whom we might know as a successful international banker or a billionaire.

According to the Preacher, riches were dangerous. They distracted people and robbed them of their softness, of their humanity. They blinded people to the realities of life and hardened their hearts. It was more difficult for a rich man to enter the Kingdom of God than for a camel to thread itself through the eye of a needle.

> Woe to you who are rich, for you have received your consolation.

> Blessed are you who are poor, for yours is the Kingdom of God. (Luke 6:24 and 20)

Jesus' sayings about wealth in the kingdom were tough and uncompromising. No material attachments. No distractions. No ties to hold the believer back. No possessions. He himself was living a simple life, with nowhere to rest or to lay his head. He expected his disciples to follow suit, to sell what they had, to give to the poor and to follow him. They were to take nothing for their journeys – no walking stick, no bag, no bread, no money. They were to leave the dead to bury their own dead because no one who put his hand to the plough and looked back would be fit for the Kingdom of God.

Allowing for a level of cultural hyperbole, in the context of the kingdom he preached, possessions had a dangerous and demonic character. They desensitised you and robbed you of the ability to listen to the summons associated with the kingdom.

According to the gospel authors, Jesus wanted his listeners to hear that the kingdom belonged to the poor in spirit, the lowly and lonely, the needy, the oppressed and destitute, to little ones, the innocent, the powerless, the victims and the blameless. The last would be first in the kingdom he preached, and the mystery of it would be revealed to little ones, to the simple and childlike. This kingdom demanded a radical, internal, spiritual transformation of attitudes and values, thereby reshaping an individual's relationship with the earth, with neighbours, with wife or husband, and ultimately with the Creator.

The Kingdom of Heaven could be compared to a man who had sowed good seed in his field and while he was not looking, one of his enemies had planted weeds among the wheat. They grew together – the wheat and the weeds. The farmer's hired hands sought his permission to clear out the weeds, but the boss was afraid some of his valuable wheat would be lost in the process. The workers would be unable to distinguish what was good and what was bad. It could all look the same. But a decision had to be made. The owner of the field was like the Creator – he was in no hurry. Everything in its own time. He would let the wheat and the weeds grow peacefully together in the same soil, and at harvest time he would instruct his men to harvest the weeds first and bundle them up to be burnt. Afterwards, they could gather his wheat and store it into the barn. The gospel writer recorded an explanation of this parable that Jesus gave to his disciples – or perhaps that teachers within the primitive community offered to their students.

The lesson was simple. The kingdom was made up of all types and it was hard to separate the good from the bad. Easy to make mistakes. Life's complicated. Don't rush in with the answers and solutions. Just let it be. In the end, a clear picture would emerge and the kingdom at work among the weeds would be refined in the process. The kingdom here on earth was not meant to be a pretty sight. The precious wheat would always be tangled up among the weeds, but in the end, once it was purified, the kingdom would look stunning.

Jesus' mind functioned in the world of farmers, of businessmen, of nature – and the world of women. He was ready to harvest some of his imagery from their domestic world. He likened the kingdom to the pinch of leaven that a woman would bury in her mass of inert dough. The world as we know it was the heap of dough – the rich and the poor, the big and the small, black and white, everybody and their institutions, companies and churches. The Kingdom of Heaven was the tiny but powerful reality that gave life and bulk, substance and significance to that world.

The Kingdom of Heaven was like a treasure hidden in a field, like a precious shimmering reality invisible in the world. When someone comes along and finds the box of treasures, he covers it up and goes away, buys the field and takes possession of an exotic collection of true gems. And again, the kingdom was like a businessman who spent his life in search of exquisite, precious stones. Finally, when his search turned up a gem of immense value, he sold everything he possessed to buy this one priceless jewel.

Jesus' kingdom demanded persistence, conviction and a willingness to make sacrifices. It was special. Its value was breathtaking and anyone with vision, any dreamer, should be prepared to sacrifice everything for the joy of being overcome by this reality.

Jesus continued to draw more and more images out of his religious imagination in an attempt to describe to his listeners the experience of being part of God's kingdom. The kingdom was like a net that a fisherman had cast into the sea and netted fish of every size and many colours. When the net was straining under the weight of his catch, the fisherman dragged it out onto the beach, sat down and sorted the tasty fish from the inedible ones. In the process of fishing, like in the business of farming, there can be no neat and clean method of separating the good from the bad while the fish are being caught, while the drama of life is being lived. All in together. No distinction. All struggling and wrestling in the same trap. In the end, no person could be the final judge of their fellows; no person could be trusted to separate the good from the bad. God's quality control was the final stage in the process and that would be the work of angels.

The challenges in the life of the kingdom: love your enemy, detach yourself from riches, turn the other cheek, indulge yourself in excesses of generosity, but no show-off behaviour, no hypocrisy or obsessive attention to meaningless details of outmoded religious practices.

The same themes keep appearing in these kingdom stories: extravagant generosity; the inclusion of the whole world in the future plan, especially the riffraff; no immediate, precipitous separation of the good, the bad and the ugly – everyone in together for the moment; the present humble reality projecting itself into the unknown future; the tragic infidelity of the Jewish people, their persecution of the prophets of God and the withdrawal of their special status as God's chosen ones.

Some modern readers, under the influence of the noble ideals of democracy and the principles of liberty, equality and fraternity, blinded by the image of what the hierarchical-monarchical Church at times became, poisoned by corruption and greed, allied to kings and dictators, are reluctant to embrace Jesus' old image of a kingdom, even of a new kingdom. A kingdom implies a king and absolute power. It involves pomp and ceremony, crowns, sceptres, thrones and privilege. A strange, foreign world of courtiers and court jesters, of courtesans and servants.

But Jesus' idea of a kingdom was something else entirely. His kingdom was to be a new reality, a whole new system of living, and being – a heaven on earth, living peacefully with one another in God's presence, breathing his air, thinking his thoughts, experiencing his love, his compassion, mixing with his children – the widows, the sinners, the lepers, the unclean, the marginalised, the blind and the deaf, the outsiders – and the women. Jesus' kingdom was to be a new world, a fresh way of interpreting our existence, a new way of looking at what is before us, around us, within us. And in this new world, under this new regime, there was to be no favoritism, no special classes, no system of priorities – no distinction between Greek and Jew, slave and free, circumcised and uncircumcised, barbarian, Scythian, male and female.

'The Kingdom' was a richly-textured, multi-layered, ambiguous, shadowy metaphor which, in Jesus' mouth, came perilously close to capturing the whole ambit of his message. Not a clear, mathematical image, but a colourful, poetic metaphor which hinted at a complex experience, at a multi-factored reality. Jesus' term 'Kingdom' points to an imaginary religious world of deep yearnings but does not fully capture the world of his message, does not mediate all its richness. This visionary world cannot be wrapped in a rigid formula of words.

The kingdom in Jesus' message encompassed the double time-frame of 'now' and 'not yet'. His kingdom was in our midst, and at the same time, it was to come, only fully realised somewhere out there in the future. This kingdom was not a sovereign territory located on a map. It was comprised of an overarching dynamic event – God taking control and coming to rule his people – a hidden process spread over an indefinite time, but one which would be completed in some kind of dramatic happening at the end of time. A process, a history, a story unfolding in a dramatic tension between the now-present and the yet-to-come: a process which God reigned over, beginning with the Creation and encompassing the whole sweep of history.

The intimate link between a Kingdom of God established in the 'here and now', in Jesus' lifetime and ours, in his actions and gestures and ours, and a kingdom to be achieved sometime in the future (who knows when – even Jesus himself did not seem to know) meant that somehow, paradoxically, mysteriously, the future reality was present in shadows, in vague outline, here and now. Present but hidden – hidden but present. The kingdom was now, but not yet, and the future Kingdom of God would be like it was then in embryo, in Jesus' lifetime, like it is supposed to be in our lifetime.

Another gospel, *The Gospel of Thomas* was discovered in 1945 in a Coptic version and as part of the Nag Hammadi Gnostic library. It is a collection of Jesus' hidden sayings and part of a strong tradition in the ancient world (Jewish, Greco-Roman and Christian) of collecting and circulating pithy sayings of prominent thinkers. This collection of Jesus' sayings was composed at some time during the second century, or even perhaps in the latter years of the first century, around the time when The Gospel of John was being put together.

Towards the conclusion of Thomas' Gospel, in *Saying 113*, Jesus' followers were asking a question that had already made an appearance in the canonical gospels, namely, when was his kingdom due to appear? In reply, Jesus told them not to look here or there, or anywhere, because 'the Father's kingdom is spread out upon the earth, and people do not see it'. The kingdom was already among them, hidden in the crevices of society. We should follow this hidden path a little further to see if we can find out what Jesus' kingdom was meant to be like, inside the seed, before it blossomed.

The gospels present the world in which Jesus ministered as a dysfunctional world of 'haves' and 'have-nots' – a world in desperate need of repair. A holy land in chaos – the Temple ruled by bankers and self-serving officials; a religion dominated by petty rules and restrictions, with legal interpretations made by religious charlatans in positions of authority, anxious to favour the rich and powerful, to burden the poor, and to keep those at the bottom of the pile in bondage; leaders interested in their own power and preferment; hypocrites feeding off the children of God.

But in God's world, men and women address him as 'Father': 'Our Father who art in Heaven'. God is the father of a crowd of beings in Heaven, the angels and the blessed, just as he is our father (and the father of all men and women) here on earth. And he will continue to be our father when we pass beyond this world of space and time. In Heaven we will be gathered together in a joyful banquet, just as we are when we celebrate the Eucharist or attend a birthday party, a wedding, or celebrate a sporting triumph, or eat with publicans and sinners, or drink with our mates in the pub, just as it was in Jesus' time, feeding the multitudes, eating in Simon's house, at the wedding party in Cana. In the kingdom, we will all share the one cup.

Our heavenly life will be what our earthly life is meant to be – a life of peace, love and forgiveness; a life in which everyone is included; a world in which priority is given to the poor, to the blind, to those who suffer – and to women of course. Brothers and sisters together, without distinction. Everyone together on the same gender spectrum. Girls equal to boys, valued in their own right. All women – sinners and prostitutes, menstruating women, foreign women, mothers (and sisters) widows (and spinsters). No wars. No hunger. No bullying. No excessive wealth and no money-power. No evil spirits – Satan's empire will be reduced to rubble.

Jesus' kingdom was to be the focus of a new gathering of humanity where the old hierarchical structures would no longer function and the categories separating one man from another would disappear. Master and servant, Jew and Gentile, black and white, first and last, rich and poor, male and female – all these distinctions are to be passé in the kingdom.

The authors of the gospels of Matthew and Luke wanted the members of their communities to remember that his apostles had invited Jesus to teach them to pray, and in prayer, to experience the presence of God as he himself did. According to the records, he was teaching his followers to address this mysterious Being not as 'Your Highness', or 'Your Eminence', or 'Your Excellency', but by the title of 'Father' or – according to the more primitive tradition of Matthew as '*our* Father – quite literally as 'our Daddy' who is 'in Heaven'. Jesus was telling his followers that they too could see themselves as the precious son or daughter of the God whom he was meeting in his prayer life. This profoundly religious prayer-experience was not an individual encounter but a family prayer for all believers, for all humankind.

With the aid of several beautifully crafted metaphors and parables, the written records show Jesus describing the unusual (some might think insane) qualities of this Being. The story of the Prodigal Father is one of his more memorable stories, and a classic in its genre. The Good Shepherd is another. Jesus the Preacher was trying to deconstruct the popular idea of God as a hard marker, as a harsh judge, by observing that no genuine father would give his child a poisonous snake or a draught of acid in answer to her request for food. By word and deed, in parables as well as by wonders, Jesus was being presented by the gospel authors as constantly revealing to his little Jewish world the face of the God he worshipped.

But what did it mean when the author of Matthew told his readers that the God Jesus had addressed as 'Father' was 'in Heaven', and that the kingdom he was preaching was also in Heaven? Was this simply meant to mean that his God and the kingdom were not on earth, that they were somewhere else, in another place, or rather not on our earth as we know it, as we see it, but in another dimension, in another order of reality – hidden, wrapped in mystery, behind a veil?

According to the story, Jesus had taught his followers to plead that their Father's kingdom should come, and to pray that his will would be done here on earth as it was done in heaven. But again, what did this mean? 'Thy kingdom come – thy will be done on earth as it is in Heaven.' What a funny thing to say! How was God's will done in Heaven? And how could any of us know? How could we know unless someone who had been there told us what Heaven was like? Did this prayer, which Jesus was teaching his followers to repeat, have any content or meaning? Was it just empty words? Just letting his followers know how important he thought the kingdom was?

If Jesus is to be accepted as a genuine preacher of his Father's message, or as the authentic revelation of some divine reality, then he would surely have known something of what happened in Heaven, of how God's will was 'done' there, how it was fulfilled in

Heaven, because, according to the records, Jesus told his followers how God wanted them to live and interact with one another here on earth. Jesus' prayer was drawing a link between how his Father's will was done in Heaven and how he wanted his followers to act out God's will here and now. The implication of course was that if they followed his lead, their life on earth would become like life in Heaven. Earth would become a mirror image of Heaven, an antechamber, a foretaste of Heaven. We know how God's will is done in Heaven because we know how it is meant to be done here on earth – or at least Jesus has given us a hint.

While the Church as we have come to know it has been intent on looking to the past and preserving the traditions, this prayer Jesus taught his apostles looks to the future. 'Thy kingdom come,' he prayed. Jesus requested his Father to guarantee that 'the Kingdom of God', 'the Kingdom of Heaven' should somehow be realised, should bud and blossom in our midst under his creative power, praying that God's will would be done, here and now, in our lives, just as it is in Heaven.

In this kingdom, at least as Jesus would have it, here and now and later in Heaven, the first would be last, and the last first. Only servants – no princes or prelates. No reserved seats or invitees of distinction. No order of knights and dames. No Eminences, or Lords, or Highnesses. Citizens of the kingdom were meant to love one another. No wars. No corruption. Little people infinitely more valuable than possessions. Everyone inside the tent and no one rejected. Men and women equal. A policy of inclusion and acceptance, no matter what our scars or rough edges, no matter whether we are blind or lame, or what genitalia we are wearing at the moment, or where our hair grows. A world for the poor, for the peacemaker, for the hungry and thirsty. Prostitutes and taxpayers included. Everyone invited to the feast. 'Blessed are the poor in spirit, for theirs is the Kingdom of Heaven.' (Matthew w5:3)

Towards the end of Matthew's Gospel, the author has Jesus outside the city of Jerusalem, sitting with his disciples, talking about the end of the world and what they could expect. To make matters clear to his readers and for the education of the members of his local community, the author spelt out in stark and dramatic terms the essence of Jesus' message about the kingdom. He recorded Jesus' colourful vision of the celebrated Son of Man coming in his glory with all his angels to separate the good from the bad, kingdom people from the others. Sheep to the right, goats to the left.

According to the story, a king appears in Jesus' vision to bless those on his right and to curse the opposition on his left. He goes on to announce the criteria by which God would judge humankind, to reward or punish those who had participated in the game of life. The king identified himself with the invisible, vulnerable people of the earth – the poor, the hungry, the thirsty, the naked and those in prison. In Jesus' dream-story, the king addresses the crowd on his right, 'Come, blessed of my Father, inherit the kingdom prepared for you from the foundation of the world.'

This king had a father who blessed and rewarded. There had been a kingdom being built and furnished for God's children 'from the foundation of the world'.

The criteria for modern Catholics for rewarding the blessed ones and condemning the cursed have changed considerably since Jesus' day. Obedience, compliance, orthodoxy, regular attendance, sexually appropriate behaviour, religious piety, a multiplicity of masses, the nine First Fridays, obsessive conformity. For Jesus none of the above applied, at least according to the Gospel of Matthew. His standards were different: care and compassion, service to others, gentleness to the weak and generosity to the needy. The kingdom would be populated by those who have fed the hungry, clothed the naked, welcomed the stranger, warmed the refugee, and visited the sick and those in prison. This rich kingdom message of the Preacher is the overall context in which Jesus' relationship with the world and with women must be viewed. With this as a background we can situate the place of women in the new creation, and within the life and ministry of the Christian movement.

CHAPTER SIX

A Woman's World at the Time of Jesus
The Cultural Setting

What was it like to be a woman in Palestine in the first half of the first century? In the far north of the country? In a little village, in Nazareth for example? A Jewish woman of any social class: a peasant, a rich lady, a member of the middle or labouring classes, a merchant's wife, a beggar or a peddler, the wife of an artisan like Jesus' mother, the daughter of a craftsman, a courtesan or street-walker?

What were the customs, the cultural attitudes, the generally accepted rules and prejudices which were wrapped around women living in a village community in the mountains, in the culture in which Jesus grew up and came to manhood? What stereotypes were circulating in his mind, pulsating in his Jewish blood? What did he see when he looked at a girl, or a middle-aged woman? How did women see themselves? What did they expect their lives to be like? What did others, the men, expect of them?

It is far from easy to drape a covering of flesh over the bare bones of a Jewish woman's life at the time of Jesus, or to describe what was probably the accepted, unreflected-upon beliefs and prejudices which cluttered the mind of someone such as Jesus living his private life in Nazareth, and later as he wandered the highways and byways of Palestine with his male companions and his female friends.

A woman's status and role in society would, of course, have depended on the mother and father the individual Jewish woman had inherited, on her brothers and sisters (if she was not an only child), on her aunts and uncles, her cousins and in-laws, where she came in the family, the status her family enjoyed in the village, what job her father did, whether her family was religious or not, how old she was – a child, a teenager, a young wife and mother, a widow, a grandmother. Many imponderables in the mix.

And much would also have depended on the mother and father who lived with Jesus and who educated him. About Joseph, the carpenter, we know next to nothing, and about Jesus' mother, only a little more. We know nothing about his extended family – his uncles and aunts, his grandparents, cousins, brothers and sisters – and next to nothing about his village. The chances are that as a boy, as a young man, he grew up surrounded by conservative folk.

The problem is further exacerbated by a serious lack of source material. So we need to tread cautiously. Nothing about Nazareth or its environs. A limited amount of material from reasonably contemporary sources such as Philo and Josephus; from classical writers of the time, such as Tacitus, Pliny and Juvenal; from archaeological sources such as the Dead Sea Scrolls or the odd inscription on a tomb. But these sources only provide some idea of women's lives and status in Rome or Alexandria, for example, or on the banks of the Dead Sea, or in Jerusalem, among the rich and famous, in the courts of King Herod. These worlds were far from the world Jesus inhabited in a tiny, isolated village. There is no door we can open to gain entrance to this rural world – no contemporary sources to draw on to paint a picture of women in his village as he and his neighbours would have known them.

We know little about the life of any single Jewish woman from Greco-Roman times – and nothing about the lives of the women in the town of Nazareth during the thirty years or so Jesus lived and worked there. Surviving sources tell us something of the colourful life of the much-married Berenice, who lived in the first century and was the mistress of the man who destroyed the second Temple (Titus), destined one day to become Emperor.

Josephus, Suetonius, Tacitus and Dio all supplied details of this lady's life. Born just before Jesus' crucifixion, around the year 28 AD, Berenice was the daughter of Agrippa and the great-granddaughter of Herod the Great; child wife of Marcus Julius Alexander (the nephew of Philo, the Jewish philosopher from Alexandria); then the wife of her own uncle, Herod of Chalis; then a widow-queen ruling with her brother Agrippa II (and probably, as the rumour spread abroad by Josephus went) sleeping in her brother's bed; then wife of the king of Cilicia, Polemo. And all this before she got together with Titus who eventually had to put her to one side when he was proclaimed emperor. At that level of society, everyone knew everyone else and was more than likely sleeping around. Fewer than six degrees separated one king from another.

As if her life was not sufficiently chaotic, Berenice was also related to the woman who reputedly had had John the Baptiser decapitated, Herodias (who had married the Tetrarch Herod Antipas even though she had been the wife of his brother Philip) and her dancing daughter, Salome.

Jesus would not of course have known the loose-living Berenice, but he might have heard of Herodias and her daughter towards the end of his life, and perhaps of their involvement in the death of his friend, John the Baptist. They were the elite living on the fringes of the Roman Empire. None of them were women with whom he would have associated.

However difficult it might be to depict the life of a female in Palestine at the time Jesus lived, we can make a few general observations that might help us understand the significance of Jesus' behaviour and appreciate what we read about his peculiar way of dealing with a variety of women – his mother, his female disciples and followers, young girls, widows, outcasts, sinners, adulteresses and wayward women possessed by demons. Fortunately, there still exist a few soft pigments on our historical palette. We can dip our brush into them and smear a few pale strokes on an old canvas. We have to try. We will never appreciate how radical and revolutionary Jesus was in his attitude towards women, in his daily contact with them, until we have made an attempt to understand their place in his society, what was expected of them, and how others viewed them.

Women in Public Life

It would be no surprise to read that in Jesus' society, like most societies throughout the history of mankind, the family unit was the engine that powered and regulated the community. In Nazareth and its surrounds, men and women, their children and extended family, worked together as a unit to secure their daily survival in an arid land. Support outside the family circle was limited – no old-age pension, no safety net or Medicare, no family benefits or child endowment, so the man of the house and his wife had to complement each other. Responsibilities within the household varied to a large extent, as you might expect, and the division of labour was mainly based on gender. The husband would perform some tasks and his wife, the mother of his children, was responsible for other aspects of their family life. She had her domain where she was in control.

It was an accepted 'truth' that women were inferior creatures. In Jesus' culture, men were the superior members of the species. Like many of the Jewish authors and commentators, like the apostles after the resurrection, as we will see, Jesus would have known that women were not allowed to preach in the synagogue or teach in schools, or carry on a business, or appear in court, or give credible evidence on behalf of a friend. One of Jesus' contemporaries, Josephus the Pharisee, had something to say about the value of a woman's testimony:

> Let not a single witness be credited, but three, or two at the least, and those whose testimony is confirmed by their good lives. But let not the testimony of women be admitted on account of the levity and boldness of their sex. (*Antiquities*, Book 4, ch.8, para. 15)

And of course, a woman could not be a member of the Pharisee Club or of the Association of Sadducees. She could not interpret the law for anyone – anyway, most of them could not read.

The Mishnah (also known as the Oral Torah, the first major written version of Jewish oral traditions) was assembled and edited by about 200 AD. It contains a saying attributed to a rabbinical scholar who had lived during the first century (and perhaps a little earlier) – more or less a contemporary of Jesus. The scholar warned his male readers against excessive contact with women:

> Yose ben Yochanan of Jerusalem says, '…don't talk too much with women'. He spoke of a man's wife, all the more so is the rule to be applied to the wife of one's fellow. In this regard did the sages say, 'So long as a man talks too much with a woman, (1) he brings trouble on himself; (2) wastes time better spent on studying Torah; and (3) ends up an heir of Gehenna'. (*The Mishnah*, tractate *Pirke Avot* 1)

In social circles in the Greco-Roman world and elsewhere, as well as in Jewish circles, respectable women were sheltered by their husbands or fathers from inappropriate public exposure. They were expected to dress modestly. Daughters were mostly confined to home under supervision for fear that they might lose their virginity, or create an unfavourable impression, thereby compromising the reputation of the head of their family. A married woman could venture abroad, but only in the company of a male relative or servant who was charged with protecting her reputation and the honour of the family, to ensure she did not do or say anything stupid or scandalous which would dishonour her family and cast a shadow over her husband or father. Women could be so unpredictable! So skittish!

The scene, however, was not uniform up and down the social scale. One can presume that the lower down the social scale you travelled, the more flexible these rules became. At the bottom of the pile, the luxury of following practices meant to ensure female propriety and reputation was somewhat reduced. So the seclusion of matrons and virgins within the home probably applied more to families who were well-off and of superior social status. For them, seclusion of their womenfolk would also have been a sign of prestige. The poor were invisible and undoubtedly freer to appear in public, to walk in the markets and visit friends. This may explain in part how Jesus was to come into regular contact with women. They were mostly members of the lower ranks.

Marketplaces, council halls, public thoroughfares, law courts, public assemblies (both civic and religious) were male-dominated domains. If women were seen in these places (and they were, as we can see from the gospels), it would have been in limited numbers – more by way of exception – and they were mostly without a voice or a vote, hidden behind a veil. The confinement of women to their domestic setting and the customs surrounding their appearance in public were associated with the family's anxiety about female virginity and the married woman's chaste behaviour, as well as being linked to hereditary and property rights.

And in the pre-modern culture in which Jesus was born and raised, women were involved in those aspects of life dealing with family and childbirth, which at that time assumed an added religious dimension. Women used to perform a variety of rituals in order to keep away evil spirits from expectant mothers and infants, or to guarantee divine blessings. This was exclusively women's work – performed by women, for women, in a woman's world. Midwives also acted as health-care workers, and played a religious role. As part of the experience of childbirth, in primitive societies, the women assisting the birthing mother offered prayers and incantations and provided potions for the birthing mother to drink. There is no reason to think the situation was any different in Nazareth or, for that matter, in Bethlehem.

It was a man's world in which women could play a minor, preferably invisible, part. They did not sit at the top of the established, institutional, hierarchical structure of the community. They were not priests, for example, or rabbis, or synagogue rulers or leaders, or Pharisees, Sadducees or lawyers. Some women, from time to time, would rise to the surface, take centre stage, assume authority, speak to the people in the name of the Lord and exercise some control by the sheer force of their personality. The sacred literature that was available in the synagogues at the time Jesus was walking the streets of Nazareth supplied examples of these exceptional women. Judith comes to mind, and Deborah, and Miriam. Being a pious Jew who attended the synagogue regularly, Jesus would have known something of these exceptional female figures.

Women also used to perform a range of semi-public functions in the local communities, as musicians, singers, mourners, midwives, prophets, sorcerers, necromancers, diviners and prostitutes, to name a few. Some of them would probably have been members of groups organised into loose, guild-type associations. For example, the 'daughters' learning dirges in Jeremiah 9:20 and wailing over Saul in 2 Samuel 1:24 were members of a guild or a company of professional mourners. Such informal organisations of women with a common interest or with shared special knowledge and expertise were part of the community life in ancient cultures of the region. These women would come together to train others and share their knowledge. They provided some essential services and gave women the opportunity to make a contribution outside the home. Jesus' mother and his sisters might have been involved in one or other of these activities.

An attentive reader (perhaps Jesus was one) could spot in the biblical literature the clear distinction between annual family religious celebrations (such as the Passover and other regular festive meals), on the one hand, and national or communal Temple and synagogue practices involving priests (always male) and community leaders such as elders and Pharisees. On the latter occasions, women were largely seen and not heard. In fact, seeing them was only just tolerated. However, women were involved in the family religious celebrations. And women used to also share in other celebrations at local shrines, and at times initiated acts of worship such as offering sacrifices or binding themselves by vow to the Lord to perform some public act.

As much as we might like to know, from this distance we cannot tell how familiar Jesus was with his people's sacred literature. We don't know, for example, whether he knew that at one stage the fierce prophet, Ezekiel, had turned his venomous tongue on a group of female prophets who were causing trouble and needed to be quelled. The prophet's condemnation was vigorous, and revealed in dazzling colour how some women had been misbehaving, what they were wearing and what they were doing – prophesying falsely, 'out of their own minds', attaching magic bands on other women, selling their fake-religious services, spreading lies, 'hunting for souls', encouraging the wicked, pretending to see 'delusive' visions and practising divination. If Jesus was familiar with the writings of the great prophets, this passage of Ezekiel might have given him a poor impression of the opposite sex …

Perhaps Jesus knew the opening chapters of 1 Samuel and the story of Elkanah, the son of Jeroham and his wife. Elkanah had travelled to the sanctuary at Shiloh to worship with his wife Hannah, his second wife Peninnah and their children. Hannah was unhappy. She hadn't been able to produce even one child for her husband. At the shrine, she had made a vow that if God blessed her with a son, she would dedicate him to the Lord. Her vow and her accompanying prayer were not proclaimed publicly. She had spoken to God in her heart.

Hannah later gave birth to Samuel and fulfilled her vow by making a sacrificial offering at Shiloh, praying publicly in praise and thanksgiving in words reminiscent of the *Magnificat* which Mary, the mother of Jesus, would later give voice to when she met her cousin Elizabeth, or at least that's the story the author of Luke's Gospel told.

Hannah was a central figure in the Jewish narrative that told the story of the birth of the prophet Samuel. However, post-biblical Jewish tradition later took steps to diminish her role. While the biblical text presented Hannah as participating actively, fully, as a major figure in public sacrifice and liturgical prayer, the later traditions tended to underplay her importance in the story.

At the time of Jesus, in summary, while women's place in society was mainly confined to the home, and while they were certainly seen as inferior to their husbands, their brothers and their sons, they did have some limited role outside, in the public domain, and the lower down the scale of social status they were situated, the more visible these women could be.

The Synagogue and Ritual Purity Prescriptions

In the Jewish culture, the number of women who were present at a meeting was not a relevant consideration when the prayer-leader was counting heads in order to form a quorum for communal prayer. They were also exempt from the obligation to pray morning and night, and from taking part in the pilgrimage to

Jerusalem to celebrate the three major feasts of the year. Nor were they required to attend the synagogue, though many of them did.

By Jesus' time, local synagogues had become the focal point of the Jewish communities and their religious observances. The Temple was a long way away, in Jerusalem, and its rituals and worship were as remote as papal masses at the Vatican. When he was at home, according to the gospels, Jesus used to attend his synagogue on the Sabbath. The gospel authors sometimes mention synagogue officials and Sabbath gatherings in the synagogue, and women were in attendance.

Each synagogue was under the control of an *archisynagogas*, or a ruler rather than a rabbi, and, in Palestine at least, this person was invariably a male. The records show that in some places outside Palestine, women could be members of the council of elders (the *gerousia*) and could make significant financial contributions to the synagogue finances, but there is no evidence of these practices in Palestine at the time Jesus was preaching and praying there.

Though the question is by no means settled, women probably occupied a separate area within the synagogue complex. Gender-segregated seating was not unknown in Greco-Roman times, in Christian churches as well as elsewhere – in theatres, for example. Philo described the situation among members of the Therapeutic society of Jews in the first century. During their communal Sabbath assembly, women and men sat in the same room, but in order to preserve the modesty of the female worshippers, a partition separated the sexes (*On the Contemplative Life*, 32-33). However, we should remember that Philo was describing the situation in his hometown, in Alexandria, not in Palestine. We don't know what was happening in Nazareth.

The female worshippers probably had to sit quietly in an area at the back of the synagogue in Nazareth, well away from the men, out of sight where they wouldn't distract or tempt God's principal worshippers. The law prescribed that women were not permitted to attend any public function for forty days after the birth of a son, for eighty days after the birth of a daughter. The birth itself, the mother's loss of blood and the extruded placenta, rendered her ritually contaminated. A woman's monthly period also made her unclean. Any object or person that a menstruating woman happened to touch – her husband, the dishes, clothing, whatever – also automatically became tainted.

Jesus would have been aware of these rules restricting a woman's participation in worship. They would have affected his mother, his sisters and female cousins and friends, and would have been as well known as the prohibitions against eating pork, or the Jewish washing rituals, or the rules regulating contact with non-Jews. They were part of the daily-weekly-monthly routine of the family.

Any contact with non-Jews, with Gentiles or Samaritans for example, also rendered the Jewish person unclean. Strangers had their own way of dealing with foods like pork, fish and reptiles, with bodily secretions, or with lepers and menstruating women, but members of the Jewish community had no control over these foreign customs, or perhaps any knowledge of them. They had to be careful. In fact, they couldn't be too careful. They had to cleanse themselves after contact before they went about their daily life, and particularly before they engaged in any form of public worship.

These rules and regulations might appear strange to a modern reader, but this system of controls and prohibitions was part of the daily life Jesus lived in Palestine. They were part of the fabric of his world. What he thought about them and the people who enforced them is another question.

Even when a man made love with his own wife, their exchange of bodily fluids rendered them both ritually impure. His semen and her bodily lubricants contaminated their happy partnership, and they were both obliged to bathe before they continued with their life. Sexual coupling, even within marriage, was a dangerous activity.

These strict purity rules that applied in the first century had little to do with any wish to avoid dirt and grime, or to get rid of the aftermath of sticky substances. Whatever their original purpose, in Jesus' time they were not really meant to ensure that a person was hygienically clean. They regulated how people related to one another and to the world around them. Some animals were regarded as unclean, so they could not be eaten. Some substances were impure – bodily secretions like sweat, spit, semen, urine, pus, vomit, faeces, tears, as well as carcasses and corpses. Some people were unclean and had to be avoided – cripples, lepers, strangers – and menstruating women. These people were not allowed to attend the synagogue services. Because of their condition, they couldn't be associated in any way with the sacred. They were somehow and for some time religiously, socially out of tune – considered by all members of the community as somehow discordant with the world above and beyond. Those afflicted with any form of ritual impurity, as women often and regularly were, were a threat to the harmony and good order of the community. They had to be avoided at all costs.

The Temple in King David's City

In Jesus' lifetime, the Temple, up there, far away in Jerusalem, remained at the heart of Jewish religious piety. At least some of those living at a reasonable distance from Jerusalem, and those fortunate enough to find accommodation in the capital city itself, would have made the effort to visit the Temple in their lifetime, maybe regularly, especially for the festivals, and would have participated in the prescribed offerings and sacrifices.

The Gospel of Luke records two occasions on which Jesus' little family visited the Temple as a family unit. Although they were living as far away from the centre of worship as any Palestinian

Jew could, the author tells us that they used to go up to Jerusalem 'every year' for the feast of the Passover; maybe that was true, not just simply a way of suggesting that they were practising Jews.

Shortly after Jesus' birth, as the story unfolds, Mary and Joseph, with babe in arms, visited the Temple to comply with the purification laws of Moses as set out in Leviticus 12 – circumcision, a period of purification for the mother and, for poor folk like Mary and Joseph, the offering of a pair of doves or pigeons.

On the second recorded occasion, Mary and Joseph had taken Jesus with them up to Jerusalem. He was twelve, and after the celebration they had left to go home, presuming that their son was somewhere, travelling with other family members on the same pilgrimage. But he had stayed behind in Jerusalem and after a heartbreaking search, they found him sitting among the teachers, listening to them and asking questions. Even at that early stage, Jesus was following his destiny – or at least, that's the picture Luke's author painted for his readers – and the Temple was the centre of learning and theological discussion.

In Jesus' time, the Temple was divided into zones that progressively restricted the public's access. The outer courtyard was open to all comers, male and female, Jew or Gentile, (except menstruating women of course, and new mothers).

The next zone was restricted to Jews of both sexes.

The third court was confined to ritually pure Jewish males, and the fourth, to ritually pure priests dressed in their proper vestments. The inner sanctuary was the exclusive domain of high priests, but only if they were appropriately robed.

In his *Wars of the Jews* (Book V, Chapter 5.2) and in *Against Apion* (2:102-4) (where he provided a more detailed description of the Temple), Josephus identified an area specially set aside for Jewish women, with gates opening onto this space reserved exclusively for them, and they were forbidden to use any of the other gates opening into the Temple.

Women used to enjoy a limited degree of involvement in the life of the Temple in Jerusalem. They could be involved in worship there, but not to the extent available to their husbands and sons. Some of the prescribed sacrifices and offerings, which were available to men, were off limits to their wives and sisters:

> Moreover, those that had the gonorrhoea and the leprosy were excluded from the city entirely; women also, when their periods were upon them, were shut out of the temple; nor when they were free from that impurity, were they allowed to go beyond the limit before-mentioned; men also, that were not thoroughly pure, were prohibited to come into the inner [court of the] temple; nay, the priests themselves that were not pure were prohibited to come into it also. (*The Jewish War*, 5.2, *The Genuine Works of Flavius Josephus, The Jewish Historian*, trans. William Whiston, 1737)

When Jesus had visited the Temple as a baby, again when he was about twelve (probably as part of his Bar Mitzvah experience), and again when he was there with his companions and had taken a whip to the money-changers, animal sacrifices were still part of the Jewish religious way of life. Though the prophets of renown had been preaching a different religious message, throats were still being cut and blood was being spilt in profusion to make Yahweh happy, and to fulfil the requirements of the Law. Jesus and his family, and his followers would have been aware of this aspect of their religious culture – bulls, goats, lambs and sheep, doves ready for slaughter. Male sacrificial animals were more valuable than females – and presumably more pleasing to God, though apparently Jesus didn't think much of the whole scene. Like the prophets before him, he was more interested in the care of widows and the poor, in visiting the sick and freeing prisoners. This regime had very little, if anything, to do with his kingdom.

The sacrificial regime described in Leviticus had been codified by the priestly school of rabbis and scholars after the exile, in the Second Temple period, and constituted the liturgy of the new Second Temple when Jesus was growing up, when he was preaching throughout Palestine, and later, when his apostles and the others were trying to spread the message and attract members from among their Jewish brothers and sisters.

The regulations dealt with a range of different ritual sacrifices – holocausts, cereal offerings, peace offerings, sin offerings and guilt offerings – and with the different categories of those who might seek to participate in a particular sacrifice. Two features of these ceremonial regulations are important.

First, while female animals were not entirely rejected as victims, at least for some of the ritual sacrifices during the Second Temple period, the sacrifices in which female animals could be presented were those of an inferior level involving only ordinary members of the community, as well as for peace or communion offerings. Members of the establishment, kings, rulers and priests had to offer male victims – bulls, rams, billygoats – animals with their gonads intact. Guilt offerings and holocausts also demanded male victims.

Leviticus sets out the ritual requirements Yahweh supposedly communicated to Moses 'when any man of you brings an offering to the Lord', and the offering is to be burnt or totally destroyed by fire. When the offering is taken from the herd, 'he shall offer a male (a bull) without blemish'; when 'his' gift is taken from the flock, from among the sheep or goats, 'he shall offer a male without blemish'.

Secondly, the hierarchical importance of sacrificial victims arranged according to the Law was a reflection of what was the situation within Jewish society in general – a hierarchy pre-ordained from the beginning in the creation of Adam and Eve. This is what constituted the background within which Jesus was educated and came to adulthood. Males of every species were obviously superior.

Adam and Eve embedded in the Jewish Psyche

The mythological story of Adam and Eve was part of the history of the Jewish nation and recited as part of its collection of sacred literature.

The story is told in the book of Genesis, a story about the formation of the first man and first woman, fashioned by the hand of God the Potter-Creator, about their initial paradise relationship and their position in the world, and about their encounter with the serpent of sin, their fall from grace and its tragic consequences. Although very little is said about them in the rest of the Old Testament literature, there they are, hand in hand, right at the beginning, in the first book of the Pentateuch, or as the Jewish people knew it, the Torah. Any Jew who attended the synagogue regularly, as Jesus did, and his mother, would certainly have known the story of Adam and his wife. Paul of Tarsus knew the story and drawing on his Pharisaical university education, he used it to refer to Jesus the Christ as the Second Adam who repaired the terrible damage the first Adam had done.

As a contemporary of Jesus (though he did not know him in the flesh), Paul was writing his letters well before the authors of Mark, Matthew and Luke had published their Gospels. He made mention in his letters of Mother Eve, and cast her in a shadowy role in the drama of history and salvation. She had succumbed to the temptation of the Serpent and as a result, because of Eve's initial flightiness, women had been unstable and easily drawn to evil.

Furthermore, according to Paul, because she had been created after Adam, God had elevated men over women. The male reflected God's glory, while the female was the reflection of her husband's glory – and naturally inferior to him.

This simple story of Adam and Eve was known to the Jews of Jesus' time. As far as we can tell from the limited records, though Jesus did not mention them by name, he was familiar with the story and used it to add weight to his opposition to divorce.

Two of the evangelists tackled this issue – the author of Mark and the author of Matthew (Mark10:1-12 and Matt 19:1ff). The perverse Pharisees wanted to expose Jesus as a charlatan. When they asked whether it was lawful 'for a man' to divorce his wife, referring to the exemption a husband enjoyed according to the Law, he agreed that Moses had allowed a man to write a certificate of divorce – but not a woman. And as Jesus is reported to have said, Moses only allowed this escape clause because of mankind's 'hardness of heart'. From the beginning, it wasn't meant to be that way. God had never intended a married couple to separate. Adam and Eve were meant for one another.

> Have you not read that he who made them from the beginning made them male and female, and said, 'For this reason a man shall leave his father and mother and be joined to his wife, and the two shall become one'? So they are no longer two but one. What therefore God has joined together, let no man put asunder. (Matt19:4-6)

Jesus was of course referring to the story in the Book of Genesis and to Adam and Eve. According to the authors, he knew the story well enough to use it as an argument to answer his opponents' question and to put them off balance. We can assume that if the event described by the authors of Mark and Matthew occurred as recorded, Jesus was as familiar as Paul with the bad reputation Eve had acquired over the years. As well as being seen as the mother of the human race and the primordial woman, she was inferior to her companion, responsible for the Fall, Adam's temptress and the agent of Satan. However, we can be sure, at least on the evidence of the Gospel narratives, that unlike Paul of Tarsus, unlike the author of the Pastoral Epistles and many of the Christian writers who followed them, Jesus did not embrace this demeaning image of Eve or this crass patriarchal view of the world. But some of his contemporaries did.

Philo was a Jewish philosopher and commentator on the Jewish Scriptures who lived in Alexandria at the time of Jesus' birth and during his public ministry in Palestine, dying about the middle of the first century. He developed a strange, allegorical interpretation of Jewish sacred literature that emerged from his interest in Greek philosophy and his wish to discover a more spiritual, less literal meaning in the Pentateuchal law. This Alexandrian thinker belongs to an ancient tradition of philosophical mystics.

Philo was to become an influential figure who touched both Jewish and Christian writers. His search for allegorical meanings was taken up, for example, by the school of Alexandrian theology, in the works of Clement and of Origen (active in the second and third centuries respectively), and later by Ambrose of Milan in the late fourth century and the other Latin Fathers who were attracted to his peculiar method of interpreting sacred texts.

In *The Hypothetica* (Eusebius, *Preparatio Evangelii* 8.5.11) Philo provided an abridged version of the constitution established in the Jewish nation by the laws of Moses. He repeated the injunction that 'wives shall serve their husbands, not indeed in any particular way so as to be insulted by them, but in the spirit of reasonable obedience in all things'. This was a command often repeated in the ancient world, repeated right up into the twentieth century, and one with which the Apostle Paul would have wholeheartedly agreed. But no such servile injunction was put into Jesus' mouth in the Gospels.

While Philo didn't explicitly set out to describe how women were to be treated and what role they were given in society and among

Jewish people at the time of Christ (no writer or thinker of that era had a mindset to dream up such an exercise), what he wrote in interpreting the Book of Genesis is illuminating. The attitudes and prejudices which rest behind his statements explain why it might have been that Jews and Christians alike were culturally unable to imagine a world in which women could assume a leadership role or exercise power outside the home, to envisage a world in which they could preach and preside at liturgical gatherings.

When God was engaged in his program of creation, he delayed to the end, to the sixth day, to fashion his prized creature – man – the perfect creature made to reflect his own image and likeness. The Creator gave man that 'admirable endowment of mind – the soul' (*On the Creation*, XXI/66).

Like many other writers of his time, Philo was fascinated with numbers, with the mystery he saw buried in them. In dealing with the Jewish creation myths and the superiority of the male member of the species, he became fixated on the number 6. (We should pause to reflect how crazy his thought processes now appear, though it has to be admitted that Philo, some of the Greek philosophers and various Gnostic teachers mark the beginning of our mathematical fascination with the universe and the search for an equation which can explain everything.)

> Of all numbers, six is, by the laws of nature, the most productive: for of all the numbers, from the unit upwards, it is the first perfect one, being made equal to its parts, and being made complete by them; the number three being half of it, and the number two a third of it, and the unit a sixth of it, and it is formed so as to be both male and female, and is made up of the power of both natures; for in existing things the odd number is the male, and the even number is the female.
>
> It was fitting therefore, that the world, being the most perfect of created things, should be made according to the perfect

number, namely, six: and, as it was to have in it the causes of both, which arise from combination, that it should be formed according to a mixed number, the first combination of odd and even numbers, since it was to embrace the character both of the male who sows the seed, and of the female who receives it.

But after all the rest, he created man, to whom he gave that admirable endowment of mind – the soul. Moses says that man was made in the image and likeness of God. (*On the Creation*, III/13-14; XXI/66; XXIII/69)

So also the first man who was ever formed appears to have been the height of perfection of our entire race, and subsequent generations appear never to have reached an equal state of perfection, but to have at all times been inferior both in their appearance and in their power, and to have been constantly degenerating. (*On the Creation*, XLIX/140)

Before Eve came onto the scene, man was living for some time in Paradise, in splendid isolation, in a garden free of disease and exempt from corruption. In the beginning, man was a pure spirit, a mind. Then at some later point, God distinguished between the sexes, making male and female, one to sow the seed, the other to receive it.

According to Philo, nothing in creation lasted forever, and all mortal things were subject to inevitable changes. The first man could not avoid disaster. With the appearance of Eve, trouble erupted.

When the first woman was created, Adam caught sight of someone closely linked to himself. He rejoiced at the sight of her and took her into his arms. Among human beings, the mind belongs to the man and is the superior, dominant element of humankind's make-up, and the sensations belong to the woman.

As a general principle, Philo had concluded that pleasure was linked to the sensations that belonged to the woman, and these sensations overpowered the male mind.

In Philo's male mind, the question had to be asked – why did the Serpent accost the woman, and not the man? Devising a treacherous stratagem against the couple, the Serpent had concluded that the woman was more prone to being deceived. Because of her softness she yielded easily. The persuasions of falsehood were able to snare her. She was unstable and frivolous, and more exposed to evil.

There you have it. According to Philo, women were to blame for bringing death, sin, corruption and disease into the world. In his worldview, they are not associated with the mind, with reason, prudence or wisdom, but with base sensations leading to pleasure, leading to 'juggleries and deceits'.

The early creation myths as told by the author of the book of Genesis to the sons of Abraham have a lot to answer for. Men's stories – dreamed up by men, told by men to men, written down by men for men. It suited those who dreamt up these myths to believe the worst of women. Nothing to do with any mysterious divine Being. All to do with the way men constructed their stories about how the world begun, and how they interpreted those stories down the ages.

In his *Hypothetica*, Philo also provided a detailed description of the communal lifestyle and ascetical practices of an isolated Jewish sect known as the Essenes – a sect which was in full bloom during Jesus' lifetime and to which his friend, John the Baptist, probably belonged for a short period. According to Philo, this sect mirrored many other clubs throughout history – 'men only' fortresses – females needn't apply. The members used to lead a celibate life free from the disturbances women inevitably bring. The reason why members didn't marry was because women were selfish creatures, 'addicted to jealousy to an immoderate degree'.

Schemers intent on undermining a man's natural inclinations, leading him astray with their Pandora's box of tricks. They are like actresses on the stage, forever composing deceitful speeches and acting out all other kinds of hypocrisy. She takes control of the 'predominant mind' of her husband by making sure he can think of nothing else while attending to her sweet talk and fluttering eyelashes. The man who is overwhelmed by the impulses of affection, who is under the influences of a woman's charms, is no longer the same person as he was. Without being aware of it, he is entirely changed. He becomes a slave instead of a free man.

Jesus ben Sirach is the final witness in the Old Testament literature to the Jewish wisdom sayings in Palestine. His collection of these sayings appeared in Palestine about 200 BC. In Alexandria, the philosopher Philo was simply expanding on his worldview: 'Sin began with a woman, and thanks to her we all must die (*Sirach* 25:24).'

The Jewish Wisdom Literature

Women are not completely absent from the pages of Jewish sacred literature – powerful women, gifted women, devious ones and influential ones. Sarah, the wife of Abraham and mother of Isaac; the Queen of Sheba, Hannah, Ruth, Rachel and Judith are a few that come to mind. Men unquestionably predominate, but from time to time a woman was seen to play a heroic role as part of God's plan. Jesus certainly would have come to know most of these female figures and heroines who formed part of his Jewish tradition.

We do not know whether in his youth Jesus was exposed to the sober maxims of his people's wisdom literature – the Book of Proverbs or *The Wisdom of Jesus the son of Sirach*, for example. Were these sacred texts used by Joseph when he was advising his son about life? Punchy aphorisms known to Joseph and planted by him in Jesus' young mind? Were the Preacher's young ears ever tuned into these streetwise admonitions? By the time Jesus of Nazareth was growing into his manhood, the Book of Proverbs and *The Wisdom of Jesus the son of Sirach* were well-settled pieces of sacred literature and included among *The Writings*. There is little cause to doubt that the Torah and the Prophets were being publicly read in the synagogue in Jesus' village, and maybe the Psalms were also being recited or sung. But no evidence is available to indicate that *The Writings*, the wisdom books, formed part of synagogal worship and were studied in the schools annexed to the synagogues. They might have been read in some places and not in others. We just don't know.

We have no direct evidence that Jesus was familiar with the nation's wisdom literature, that he had read it, or even scanned some of its passages. The Book of Proverbs and *The Wisdom of ben Sirach* in their final forms had been available in Palestine from about 130 BC – almost certainly in Jerusalem and in the halls of learning – available to scholars and members of the hierarchy. But we don't know whether copies of these wisdom books had travelled as far north as Nazareth.

In the first century of the Christian era, many configurations of the faith and practices of Judaism were at play in Palestine and in other parts of the world. The Jewish religion as we have come to know it was not yet a centralised, homogenous feature of life. Jewish sects differed significantly throughout the land, in theology and practice. Service in an isolated synagogue in Nazareth would have been different from the services in synagogues in and around Jerusalem, from services in other parts of Galilee or throughout the Diaspora. The movement to co-ordinate and unify the Jewish theology and practices did not begin until the second century.

However, even if Jesus had not read and studied the wisdom literature, it can still serve as witness to cultural attitudes and prejudices in the world in which he grew up, and can provide a good indication as to how women were thought of by religious Jews in the first century. In any event, there are some signs that as a mature man, Jesus was not unfamiliar with the ideas and insights which appear in these texts – the down-to-earth, common-sense advice of a wise man in determining man's destiny, in facing life's challenges, dealing with crises and anxieties, resolving daily ambiguities.

According to Matthew and Luke's Gospels, Jesus was a wise man after the style of the ancient sages, a gifted exponent of the values, the principles and literary techniques of Palestine's wisdom literature. He spoke of the tension between God and money, of judging others, of earthly and heavenly treasures, of treating others as one would want to be treated, of rich men struggling to fit through the eye of a needle, of Providence and much more – all well-known themes of the Wisdom literature:

> Let me give you this advice. Don't be too worried about your life, what you shall eat or what you shall drink, or about your body, what you shall put on. (Matt 6:25ff)*

He spoke of the birds of the air, of the lilies of the field and of King Solomon in all his glory. A careful reader of the gospel literature can pick up echoes of the Jewish wisdom literature behind the Jesus words as they were reported by the gospel writers.

If these gospel passages reflect what Jesus was truly like, whatever we can say about the Book of Proverbs or the words of his namesake, the son of Sirach, somewhere he had clearly been exposed to the wisdom tradition of his people and had made it part of his religious mindset and vocabulary.

The author of the Book of Proverbs painted a portrait of the ideal Jewish woman. She was, of course, a wife – subservient, obedient, full of domestic energy and a strict governess in her little world. According to him, a good wife was difficult to find, and far more precious than any jewel. She would be out of bed before sunrise, providing food for her family and a list of tasks for the maids.

A real wife could be relied on. Her lamp was never extinguished – even at night. Always walking the corridors, in and out of every room of the house, attending to the least detail. A dutiful wife was the root and branch of a man's pride before the world. Her husband would glory in his reputation at the gates of the city where he could sit confidently among the elders of the land, the successful businessmen and scholars, and enjoy his wealth and his wife.

In addition to her pivotal role in giving birth and providing for the continuation of the family, a good woman has always enjoyed an important (and sometimes dominant) domestic role. Within the home, she would attend to the economic, educational and some of the religious needs of the family members. She grew crops, cultivated gardens and kept domestic animals – sheep, goats, and chickens. She processed food: soaking, grinding, pickling, drying, roasting, churning, baking bread and preparing meals. She made clothes: spinning, weaving, and sewing. She even potted plants. Since these activities usually involved women from the neighbouring households, they created informal social networks of support, especially in times of stress or illness.

We can assume that Jesus and his mother were also part of the daily routine of their village. Except perhaps for his encounter with Peter's mother-in-law, the Gospels don't record incidents of Jesus' contact with what we might call ordinary women – wives and mothers in their domestic setting – shopping in the markets, cooking in the kitchen, at table with the family. We can assume, however, that he had had daily contact with many such women in and around Nazareth while he was growing up and working in the area.

In contrast to his description of the 'good wife', the author of the Book of Proverbs had a jaundiced view of the troublesome, nagging, quarrelsome woman. According to him, some women were foolish, noisy and annoying. They knew no shame. Some would sit at the door of their house or take a seat on the high places of the town, calling out to those who were passing by, looking to entrap any young, stupid, innocent man.

In other parts of the Book of Proverbs, the author described the lifestyle and behaviour of sinful women, harlots and harridans, who went about causing trouble in the community, leading young men astray. He offered his young readers this advice:

> "Listen carefully, my friend, and treasure what I am about to tell you. You must treat my teachings as the apple of your eye and write them on the tablet of your heart. My advice will keep you safe from the temptations of a woman of loose morals, from the allurements of her sweet, smooth words."*

The author imagined himself looking from the window of his house, watching a silly young man, devoid of any common sense, under the control of his instincts. He sees him passing along the street near the corner, taking the road to a house of ill repute. The author watches a woman approaching and engaging this young man in conversation. She is dressed like a prostitute. Loud and frivolous. Wisdom knows that this kind of woman is always 'on the make', out on the streets, in the marketplace, never at home where she should be. She is lying in wait at the corner. The author described the scene. She seizes the stupid young man and kisses him hard on the lips, puts her hand in sensitive places and invites him home.

> I'm ready for you. I have decked my couch with coloured spreads of Egyptian linen. I have perfumed my bed with myrrh, aloes, and cinnamon. Come let us take our fill of love till morning. Let us delight ourselves with love. My husband is not at home, so we can be alone.*

Very enticing. How could he resist? Taking him by the hand and with her sweet talk, she forces him to follow. An ox on his way to the slaughter, a stag about to put his hoof in a trap, a bird gliding into a snare. This woman has had many customers over the years. A mighty troop of stupid men – trophies for her mantelpiece. Off he goes with her to 'the chambers of death'.

The editor of these maxims and images warned his young male pupil to avoid kissing a shameless, lustful woman because her lips dripped honey, and her words were soft and oily. In the end, when she had finished with him and thrown him on the scrapheap, he would learn that this female jezebel was as bitter as wormwood and as sharp as a two-edged sword. Whatever she might say, and however attractive she might appear to an eager young man, he should not go near her door. If he did, he would inevitably be fatally tempted to enjoy her offerings and waste his life. All his energy would be wasted rutting – tilling the land of his enemy.

Maybe at some critical stage of his adolescent life, Joseph (or some rabbi of the town) provided similar advice to Jesus. If he was familiar with the wisdom literature, the negative attitudes and chauvinist fears, the anti-feminine prejudices behind the wisdom words did not seem to have contaminated his mind. The Jesus we meet in the gospels never uttered a harsh word to a woman, or about women, or offered young men any advice to poison their minds against women of ill-repute.

The Book of Proverbs is full of advice on everything under the sun – how to raise and discipline children; how to deal with fools; when to remain silent; about self-control and gossip; about weighing what you hear and not accepting everything uncritically; discernment, wisdom and friendship; wine, dinner parties – and we can find spread through the text, hard-nosed, practical advice about women.

According to the author, no wickedness comes anywhere near the wickedness of a woman. A man's bad temper is preferable to a woman's kindness. The author claimed that he would rather deal with a lion or a dragon than live in the same house with a wife filled with bile. A woman's spiteful fit changes her looks. Her face takes on the grim appearance of an ugly bear.

'Do not be taken in by a woman's beauty – never lose your head over a woman.' A man should never deliver up his soul to any woman, or allow her to trample on his strength. He shouldn't keep company with prostitutes in case he becomes entangled in their snares. He should not dally with singing girls, nor stare at virgins, or prowl around in unfrequented streets. A man has to turn his eyes away from a handsome woman. He should steel himself not to stare at the beauty that belongs to another man – to her husband. He should never sit down with a married woman or enjoy a glass of wine with her in case he succumbs to her charms.

'A woman's beauty has led many astray. It kindles desire like a flame.' The Jewish poet who wrote *The Sentences* sometime within a hundred years either side of the changeover to the modern era (and who pretended his advice was the work of the ancient Greek poet Phocylides), advised his young reader not to prostitute his wife by letting other men sleep with her. The reason for this sophisticated piece of wisdom, however, had nothing to do with the innate value and dignity of his partner or the transparent beauty of their relationship. A man should not pollute his genetic line and encourage his wife to produce bastards. The father of the family should strive to keep his bloodline unadulterated otherwise the legitimacy of all his children would be suspect. And Jesus ben Sirach was reading from the same page. He thought that a wife's adulterous liaison was an offence against the law of the Most High, an offence against her husband as well as a stain on the children upon whom punishment would fall. Both Philo and Josephus also condemned any wife who was sleeping around – because they deprived their husbands of legitimate heirs, which was one of the principal roles God had entrusted to females.

The relationship between a father and his daughter received a good deal of treatment from the pen of Jesus of Sirach and a more than passing reference among the maxims in *The Sentences*.

The accepted wisdom of ben Sirach was that a daughter kept her father awake with constant worry. When young, in case no one would want her and she would be condemned to gather dust on his shelf; when a virgin, in case someone would get at her and she would be defiled, with an unwanted child in her father's house; when married, in case she didn't please her husband, or in case she was barren, or she strayed into the arms of a stranger. A father had to keep a keen lookout and maintain control over his headstrong daughter in case she made him a laughing-stock and she became the object of gossip in the village. No matter her age or marital status, a daughter was the cause of stress and anxiety in case she compromised her father's reputation. No sleep for the fathers of daughters.

> Keep strict watch over a headstrong daughter lest, when she finds her freedom, she uses it to wound herself. Be on guard against her wandering gaze, and do not wonder if she sins against you. As a thirsty wayfarer opens his mouth and drinks from any water near him, so will she sit in front of every post and open her quiver to the arrow. (Sir 26:10-12)*

Or as the Good News translation turned the Greek Septuagint text into modern English, 'She'll spread her legs anywhere for any man who wants her, just as a thirsty traveller will drink whatever water is available.'

The reader was also advised not to 'touch' his stepmother or his father's mistresses because they belonged to his father, not to him. By presuming to couple with his father's second wife or his concubine, a son was violating his father's rights and privileges. The poet's Jewish heritage shone through these prohibitions. The Pentateuch recorded a litany of commands forbidding sexual concourse with a range of people, male and female, including stepmothers and mothers-in-law – and animals to boot. Reflecting on the state of the union among the Jews, Ezekiel dipped his pen in purple ink and let fly:

> You have despised my holy things, and profaned my Sabbaths. There are men in your community who slander to shed blood, and men among you who eat pagan sacrificial flesh upon the mountains. Men are committing lewd acts in your ranks. Some of your men uncover their fathers' nakedness and humble women who are unclean in their impurity. One commits abomination with his neighbour's wife; another lewdly defiles his daughter-in-law and another of your men defiles his sister, his father's daughter. (Ezek 22:8-10)*

The world of lechery and debauchery revealed in the prescriptions of Leviticus and railed against by the prophet Ezekiel was not the world Jesus inhabited with his followers, as least as described by the authors of the four gospels. Nonetheless, Leviticus was part of the Jewish Pentateuch and Ezekiel one of the three major prophets. Both were part of the canon of sacred books that were opened regularly in the synagogue at Nazareth and read aloud. Although these were language and laws with which Jesus and at least some of his followers were undoubtedly familiar, they find no place in the gospels. As far as we know from those four books, Jesus did not go near the tangled, twisted world of sex except to say that anyone who stared hard at a woman with his head full of lust and lechery had already committed adultery with her in his heart.

Whether these works of literature were part of Jesus' education, whether they provided the basis of Joseph's paternal advice to his young son will never be known. However, we can be confident that the attitudes and principles hidden in the Jewish wisdom literature reflected the culture of the times and provided the background against which we can assess Jesus' life and teachings. They provide a context in which we can see how radically different his attitudes towards women were.

Marriage and Divorce

There was no technical term in the sacred literature to describe the institution of 'marriage'. The bond created between a man and a woman was captured by the simple statement that a man 'took' a woman as his partner or wife, and the passive voice was used for the woman. She was 'taken' by the man into his extended family. She would pack her belongings and move into his family's house, join in his family's activities, beget his children, care for and educate them in unison with other members of the household, prepare food, bake, weave and sew.

And the Bible doesn't record any explicit 'marriage laws'. From the various stories told and retold, however, we can conclude that as a general rule most brides' families provided a dowry and that this property (jewels, clothing, utensils, and for rich parents, livestock or servants) remained the wife's possessions, at least in principle.

At the time of the 'taking', the groom's family would make a betrothal gift to the girl's family. This ancient custom has sometimes been interpreted as a price paid for the bride. She became her husband's property. He had bought her and could treat her as part of his chattels.

These betrothal and dowry payments together served important economic, social and legal functions in agrarian and primitive communities. An ownership-chattels interpretation of these customs, however, does not reflect the true, more nuanced relationship between the families involved. Talking about a wife being the property of her husband was only half-true. It tended to trivialise the relationship between a father and his daughter, between a man and his wife, and really missed the point.

The betrothal gift provided some compensation to the wife's family for the loss of their daughter's services within her birth family. The dowry, on the other hand, was to provide the bride's principal means of support if her husband were to die or divorce her. In agrarian communities and villages, these exchanges of gifts established alliances between families that might prove mutually advantageous at times of financial stress.

We know nothing about how these practices applied in the case of Mary and Joseph. Their engagement and marriage arrangements read as though they were not formalised in any traditional sense. Maybe in Jesus' social circle up north, especially among the not-so-rich, the customs and practices were more informal, or perhaps non-existent.

In his book *Contra Apionem*, writing in the period some forty or so years after Jesus' death, Josephus the Pharisee recorded something about his people's laws on marriage:

> The law commands us also, when we marry, not to have regard to the amount of the dowry, nor to take a woman by violence, nor to persuade her deceitfully and knavishly; but to demand her in marriage of him who hath power to dispose of her, and is fit to give her away by the nearness of his kindred; for, says the Scripture, 'A woman is inferior to her husband in all things.' Let her be obedient to him; not so that he should abuse her, but that she may acknowledge her duty to her husband; for God hath given the authority to the husband.

> Moreover, the law enjoins that after the man and wife have lain together in a regular way, they shall bathe themselves; for there is a defilement contracted thereby, both in soul and body, as if they had gone into another country. By being united to the body, the soul is subject to miseries, and is not freed from these miseries except by death. For this reason the law requires purification to be entirely performed." (*Contra Apionem*, Bk 2 Ch. 25)

Josephus might have believed that the Scriptures stated that a woman was inferior to her husband in all things. If he did, he was wrong. He was leading his readers into error. And he thought that engaging in sexual activity was like going into a foreign country, getting dirty in soul and body, and being miserable until we are liberated by death. In this regard, many bishops, monks and theologians would agree, though we have no evidence that Jesus did.

Men and women, husbands and wives were not equal in the family or in the community at large. This was apparent, *inter alia*, in the realm of sexuality. A woman's sexuality was strictly controlled by her father and brothers before her betrothal, by her husband afterwards. In Jesus' culture, as in many others, land was all important and ownership was transferred through the male members of the household, so the husband had to ensure the paternity of any children his wife might produce.

Consequently, a strict system of law was developed to protect and guarantee the virginity of girls before they were 'taken' to their husband's family. The sexual integrity of any bride was prized beyond telling.

Men and women were also treated differently according to the biblical laws dealing with adultery. For example, sex between a married man and an unmarried woman was frowned on, but was not forbidden, whereas a married woman who committed adultery by having sex with anyone other than her husband could expect no mercy – straight to the pit where the male participants were supplied with a pile of chaste stones and expected to do their duty. This arcane law was based on a man's property rights rather than any idea of sexual morality. A wife and her reproductive powers belonged to her husband.

If a man slept with another man's wife, both offending parties could expect to be punished – a death sentence for both.

Otherwise, a man could play around and do what came naturally to him, but a woman had to preserve herself for her future husband, or if married, be ready to welcome the exercise of his exclusive rights to her body.

A girl's physical integrity was a priceless gem that was considered essential to establish and maintain the honourable status of her father or husband. According to the law, her body belonged to the dominant male of her family. Her husband could touch her and probe her private parts, but no one else. He could do what he liked, but it was a slur on him (on him, not on her) if some other man were to enjoy her body. Adultery was an offence against the husband. He could wander, philander any unmarried woman, young or old, with impunity, but if his wife were to stray, the penalty for her and her lover was death.

Divorce was another area of the Jewish law where women were discriminated against, though how much this aspect of society touched Jesus is far from clear. There is some hint in Matthew's Gospel (1:19) that for a time Joseph considered separating from Mary (or putting her away quietly), but this was before Jesus' birth and as far as we know, the prospect never surfaced again.

The Mishnah dealt with marriage contracts and the behaviour of married women. If a woman transgressed the Law of Moses and the Jewish law, on termination of her marriage, she was not entitled to any payment under the contract. To illustrate, the Mishnah provides three examples of a wife breaking the Jewish law. First, if she went out with her hair flowing loose; secondly, if she were to conduct her spinning duties out in the marketplace, in public; and thirdly, if she spoke to 'just anyone', indiscriminately, or held a conversation with men, or engaged in loose talk', in gossip. However, in quoting the Mishnah, we should be aware that the recording of an opinion of a particular rabbi is not necessarily evidence of the fact that he had actually expressed that interpretation of the law, or if he had, whether what he said was a true reflection of a view generally prevailing among rabbis, or of a socially accepted practice.

At one stage of his public life, challenged by lawyers and Pharisees, Jesus addressed the question of divorce and appears to have known something of the law. Though the laws dealing with divorce were not set out in the sacred texts, the Book of Deuteronomy leaves us with the unavoidable impression that a man could put away his wife for some physical inadequacy or blemish – for example, by giving her a 'bill of divorce', but the wife was powerless in the face of an offending or offensive husband. The presumption seems to have held true in Jesus' time.

> And Pharisees came up to him and tested him by asking, 'Is it lawful to divorce one's wife for any cause?' He answered, 'have you not read that he who made them from the beginning made them male and female, and said, 'For this reason a man shall leave his father and mother and be joined to his wife, and the two shall become one'? So they are no longer two but one. What therefore God has joined together, let no man put asunder.' They said to him, 'Why then did Moses command one to give a certificate of divorce, and to put her away?' He said to them, 'Because of your hardness of heart Moses allowed you to divorce your wives, but from the beginning it was not so. And I say to you: whoever divorces his wife, except for unchastity, and marries another, commits adultery; and he who marries a divorced woman commits adultery.'
> (Matt 19:3-9)

This interchange between Jesus and the Pharisees gives some force to the general belief that a husband owned his wife and could treat her as part of his property. But according to Jesus it had not always been so. It had been different from the beginning and in the mind of the Creator. Mysteriously, surprisingly, the law had changed. God's original plan had been modified to make some allowance for a man's 'hardness of heart'. In our broken world, there has to be some wriggle-room for the weak. As Philo had observed, nothing is perfect under the sun, though when God had created man and woman, he meant them to live together as a unit, as a team, in harmony. He never meant the husband to have any unfair advantage over his partner that would allow him to put her aside if he saw fit. But exceptions had to be made (at least according to Jesus) because men had proved too weak to maintain the original arrangement. However, in the Kingdom of Heaven, husband and wife should return to the original plan based on love and fidelity. In the matter of divorce, men had no advantage. They were bound by the same regime as their wives. Jesus was having nothing of his people's lax policy of gender inequality that favoured men.

Female Education

We don't know what proportion of any community in Palestine in the first century could read or write. We can say with some degree of certitude that those who could read were more numerous by far than were the writers, but even that basic skill was limited. It's more than likely that Mary had never been taught to read or write.

In those days, formal education was a function of a family's social status, the availability of schools for the young (and so a family's proximity to centres of learning like Rome, Alexandria or Jerusalem), and of course, gender – whether we are talking of boys or girls. The rich had a better chance than the poor – and it was ever thus! As in Australia today, if you lived in a city you had measurable advantages over bush folk. Young males were significantly ahead of girls. All the available evidence suggests that in the Greco-Roman world generally (and as it existed in

Palestine), as well as in the Jewish culture, by a significant degree, far fewer women learnt to read or write. The vast majority of women received little to no formal education over and above what their mothers taught them about keeping house – cooking, sewing, growing crops, spinning and weaving. Education was just another sign of a girl's inferiority to her brothers, a wife's to her husband.

The Lot of a Female Slave

The image of himself which Jesus prized was that of a slave – and a pagan slave at that, since Jewish slaves in Jewish households were not required to stoop as low as to be feet-washers, as Jesus was at his farewell supper. And Jesus instructed his disciples that they had to follow his lead and agree to wash the feet of all comers.

Slavery was part and parcel of the world to which Jesus belonged. The author of Luke's Gospel narrated the story of Jesus conversing with a Roman soldier who had approached him to intervene on behalf of his mortally ill slave. The author of Matthew briefly mentioned the slave of the high priest who had had his ear sliced off in the melee surrounding Jesus in Gethsemane Garden and whose appendage Jesus had miraculously re-attached. A little later, according to the Passion story, Peter had found himself outside in the courtyard while the troops were interrogating and torturing Jesus, when a female slave (a maid-servant) had approached him and accused him of being one of the associates of Jesus the Galilean.

Slaves were members of the early Christian communities that Paul had established. In his letters he used to give words of encouragement and guidance to slaves and their owners. Slaves were advised to be respectful and obedient, while their masters were warned to be merciful and kind towards those under their control.

Slaves were also part of the imaginary figures that inhabited Jesus' world. They made their way into a number of his parables and sayings. He counselled his followers to be ready and waiting, loins girded, lamps burning, expecting the son of man to appear out of nowhere, unexpectedly, and to behave like slaves waiting for their master to return from a wedding feast. According to the author of Matthew, Jesus once compared the performance of two slaves – one fulfilling his master's orders when he was left in charge of the household and attended to the meals of the family, and the other, a lazy drunk who would beat his fellow slaves whenever his master was away.

Like prostitution, female slavery was an ugly fact of life in Jesus' time – and taken for granted as part of the landscape. He and his apostles would have been familiar with the institution of slavery in their society and Jesus may have observed signs of it even as he was growing up in Nazareth. The rich and famous of the region would have enjoyed the services of slaves, both male and female. They were part of the Greco-Roman world, even among the Jewish people, the valuable property of their owners, ready to obey their commands and to supply their every need. Female slaves would have done the shopping in the marketplace for their mistresses, the house-cleaning, as well as providing sexual services on demand for their masters.

In Summary

The disadvantages experienced by women in Palestine at the time Jesus was living were a function of two separate traditions: the role of and attitudes to women as developed within the Jewish culture over centuries, and the place of women in the larger Greco-Roman world, which was based on accepted gender differences and on a hierarchical-patriarchal societal structure.

In Palestine of the first century, a woman's place was in the home – mother and manager, responsible for rearing and educating children. It may have been somewhat different in some circles in Corinth, in Alexandria or Rome, even in a Greco-Roman family in Palestine, but Jesus was a Jew, a pious, practising Jew, as his mother and father had been. He lived as a teenager and young adult in a village in the north of the country, and later travelled from village to village, almost always in a Jewish setting, preaching and wonder-working, visiting the capital city of Jerusalem, probably on several occasions, to celebrate the feasts.

He was living and breathing each day in a world in which women were inferior, appearing in public only in the company of a male chaperone – not visible and not heard. They could not be seen running a business or earning a living outside the home. A mother and her daughter were a husband's responsibility. He had control within the family and his women-folk had to be obedient and submissive.

A daughter whose father died before her marriage, and any impoverished widow, had to rely on the good graces of their nearest male relatives or else beg on the street or go into prostitution. No social security for abandoned widows. No safe-houses for battered wives and mothers.

Jesus' world was basically a man's world. The males enjoyed social respect and honour in their own right, but females drew their status and respect from their father, from their husband or some other close male relative. Women were destined to bask in the glory of their male sponsor. They were expected to protect their family honour by behaving properly – to dress appropriately, to cover their heads and hide their hair, to remain silent in public and speak to men only when spoken to – and then only to a relative. This male-dominated world was considered completely normal by those walking around within it – by the men and the women. This was the world in which Jesus lived and worked.

CHAPTER SEVEN

'Not Counting Women and Children'

While according to the evidence, Jesus might have had an original, unconventional attitude to women and children in his life and work, this does not necessarily mean that his views translated smoothly into the lives and attitudes of his followers, including the authors of the gospel records. After all, the image of his apostles and male disciples as depicted in the gospel literature is one of a band of pretty dense men – slow to understand, dragging their feet in their Teacher's puzzling world. Jesus might have been enlightened (and there is no doubt he was), but the composers of the gospels might have remained trapped in the mentality of their age and culture, telling stories about Jesus which revealed a novel way of looking at women, but inadvertently, unconsciously, in a passing comment or a throwaway line, providing evidence of having feet set in the dry concrete of their society.

The four gospels tell the story of Jesus feeding a hungry crowd of listeners by multiplying a few loaves and fishes. In fact, for some reason Matthew and Mark tell the story twice.

As the authors recorded the details of this event, they recalled that Jesus' disciples were responsible for controlling the crowd and distributing the food. At least in the Gospel of Luke, the Greek term for 'disciples' included both men and women, and as we will see, and since women formed a part of the Jesus' travelling team, it is likely that they were also distributing the food.

However, in reporting the number of those who had been served, the author of one of the gospels (Matthew's) provides a momentary insight into society's attitude to women. The reader has to concentrate or she would miss it. The reports in all three Synoptic Gospels and in John's state that Jesus had fed four or five thousand 'men' or 'people' (most languages, modern and ancient, unless the author otherwise specifies, include women in the generic collective word 'men'), but in both his account the author of Matthew's Gospel added 'not counting women and children'. The author of John's Gospel also provides one small but significant detail. He recorded that a small boy or a child had been present at the event and that he was carrying five barley loaves and two fish. If this detail is historically accurate, boys (and presumably girls) formed part of the contingent that was following Jesus around on his preaching peregrinations.

'Not counting women and children.' This throw-away remark probably reflects the social structure and mentality of the times – a mentality that Jesus did not share – in fact one that he took steps to undermine. Such a casual, unreflective remark can have buried within it a maze of social values and attitudes.

Why were women and children not counted? Overlooking women and children was clearly contrary to the implicit policy of Jesus, at least as he was depicted by the four gospel writers. The Jesus described in the early Christian literature wouldn't have made such an off-handed remark. In his world, everyone was counted and countable – women and children, prostitutes and tax collectors. But the author of the narrative seems to have remained unconsciously hamstrung by convention. He made his remark without explanation, as though his readers would have immediately understood and not needed to look for a reason why only men were being counted.

To appreciate the invisible power of this remark, imagine a world in which a storyteller was to state that there were present at some meeting '4000 children, not counting men and women', 'not counting parents' or '4000 women, not counting men and children'. Both statements would invite probing questions, and demand an explanation. Why only count women? Maybe because it was a woman's convention called to discuss women's business. Or, it was a children's festival and the reader needed to know how many children had attended – and even then, there would be no need to mention the adults. But in any event, there would have to be some plausible explanation proffered before these simple statements would feel right.

But no explanation was required when the number of men present was recorded – 'not counting women and children'. The simple statement was sufficient. The author of the narrative was simply reflecting the status quo. That was the way society was.

But the Jesus described for us in the gospel stories would not have been happy. Children were part of the kingdom. They were important and fully embraced:

> Let the little children come to me. Don't stop them, whatever you do. Let them come. Unless you become like these little children, you can't enter the kingdom. Those who are travelling towards the kingdom have to model their lives on children and achieve the simplicity, the unquestioning trust and complete dependence everyone associates with little ones. (Mark 10:13f, Matt 19:13f, Luke 18:15f)*

Children were not to be invisible among the kingdom people. They were not fringe-dwellers in the Kingdom of Heaven.

As we will see, women too were part of his small group of followers, fully paid-up members of his team, loved, cherished and respected. Everyone, big and small, young and old, male and female, Jew and Gentile was counted – even slaves.

This offhanded, throwaway remark of the author of Matthew casts into relief the significance and weight of the many gospel passages featuring women, and perhaps explains why it was, in the early church, when its structures and authority positions were being established and defended, the gospel composers/editors decided, consciously, or more likely, unconsciously, to include material which would booster the vocation and position of male followers rather than female.

However you look at the theological, historical evidence and at the priority the early Christian writers gave to men, the early church believed that women of all types and ages were at the centre of Jesus' life. He had mixed freely with all kinds of women – not just with his female relatives, but with young women and women on the fringe of society – and they had responded warmly to him and his message. He had treated them as real persons, not as property. We will see him engaging with them in deep spiritual conversations, with the Samaritan woman by the well, for example, with Mary the sister of Martha, and later with Mary Magdalene after the resurrection, talking about personal, spiritual matters. And, perhaps to the disappointment of bishops and priests, we do not read about Jesus discussing these matters so openly, so freely, with his male companions and disciples. A tradition was to develop in the second and third century prioritising women as prophets and suggesting that Jesus had revealed secret messages to his friend Mary Magdalene and that some of his apostles had become jealous – and hostile.

According to the Gnostic Gospel of Mary (re-discovered at the end of the nineteenth century but probably written sometime in the second century), Mary Magdalene had apparently been the focus of some division and ill will in the early Christian community. She was the person who had stood up to Peter and Andrew, and who had challenged their authority. In this Gospel, when the members of the community had begun to discuss the Saviour's message, Peter invited Mary (almost certainly Mary Magdalene) to share her special knowledge with them. She had been specially privileged during Jesus' life. He had shared secrets with her.

> Sister, we know that the Saviour loved you more than all other women. Tell us the words of the Saviour that you remember, the things which you know, that we don't know because we didn't hear them.

Mary replied by recalling a conversation about her visions which she had had with Jesus, but her vision and her revelation did not please some of the brothers, Andrew and Peter particularly. Addressing his brothers and sisters, Andrew remarked, 'Say what you like about the things she has said, but I do not believe that the Saviour said them. These teachings are strange ideas.'

As the story was told, Peter joined in to express his concerns, 'Did he, then, speak with a woman in private without our knowledge about it? Are we to turn around and listen to that? Did he prefer her over us?'

Mary was upset. The male apostles were casting a shadow of doubt over her authenticity and over her right to speak. She burst into tears and said, 'My brother Peter, what are you imagining? You think that I have thought up these things by myself in my heart or that I am telling lies about the Saviour?'

Then the apostle Matthew intervened with a startling put-down. For any contemporary Christian who is familiar with Peter's established position within the little apostolic group, with how the authors of the canonical Gospels attempted to prop up his authority and primacy, his status in the primitive community, and how his successors have prized their link to Peter, expanding their institutional control over the universal Church, Matthew's contribution to this unpleasant confrontation is surprising, maybe even scandalous. He was putting Peter and the other apostles back in their place:

> Peter, you have always been a wrathful person. Now I see you contending against the woman like the evil spirits. For if the Saviour made her worthy, who are you to reject her. Assuredly,

the Saviour's knowledge of her is completely reliable. That is why he loved her more than us. We should be ashamed. We should clothe ourselves with the perfect Human, acquire it for ourselves as he commanded us, announce the good news, not laying down any other rule or law that differs from what the Saviour said.

The failure to count the women and children as suggested, *en passant*, by the author of Matthew may seem a tad trivial, but it did reflect what we know to have been the attitudes of the times towards women, and it suggests that those in charge of making the count and recording it were themselves infected to some extent with the social disease of female invisibility.

CHAPTER EIGHT

Jesus' Female Followers

Whoever composed Luke's Gospel wanted his readers to know that Jesus was the type of wandering preacher who had female followers in his team. As he told the story (Luke 8:1ff), soon after he had eaten with Simon the Pharisee and the elite of the town, he continued his campaigning in the north, through cities and villages, preaching his message of the kingdom. The twelve were travelling with him and 'some women who had been healed of evil spirits and infirmities': Mary Magdalene who had been delivered of seven demons, Joanna, the wife of Chuza who was Herod's steward, Susanna and 'many others' who were providing for him and his retinue from their own purse. As the wife of the manager of Herod Antipas' estate, Joanna would have been a woman of influence and wealth. Sometime previously Mary Magdalene had apparently been on a wild trip, but she had now settled down in Jesus' band of followers.

These many women may have been accepted by Jesus as his disciples, but no special word existed in the language Jesus was speaking, to describe them as his pupil disciples. If only because the rabbinical schools enrolled male students, not female, the word for a disciple, in both Hebrew and Aramaic, existed only in its male form. There had been, at least until Jesus came along, no demand for the feminine variety. The author of the Acts of the Apostles (the same man who had composed the Gospel of Luke) would use the Greek word for 'disciple' in its feminine form, *mathetria*, to describe Tabitha as a 'discipless' living and working within the primitive community at Jaffa. She was said to be 'full of good works and acts of charity'; what a modern translator might (anachronistically) describe as a female deacon.

Perhaps Jesus didn't explicitly number any of his 'many women' followers among his team of disciples. We have to wait until the second century and the apocryphal *Gospel of Peter* (12/50) before the title 'disciple', in its singular and feminine form (*mathetria*), would be applied to a woman who had been associated with Jesus in his public ministry – to someone who had been a prime witness to his resurrection. In the apocryphal and gnostic writings of the second and third centuries, Mary Magdalene would appear as a favourite and influential 'disciple' of Jesus. Some centuries after the historical events of Jesus' life, Mary Magdalene would even become known as 'the apostle of the apostles' (*apostolorum apostola*) and in the apocryphal literature, she would be elevated to legendary status. However, before being admitted into the company of the angels in heaven, she would have to be 'transmogrified' back into the original, perfect specimen of human beings – a male like Adam and Jesus.

But putting to one side for the moment the question as to whether the descriptive title 'disciples' included some women, it is clear, from Luke's Gospel especially (but also from other passages), that the gospel authors did include women among Jesus' disciples. Women were on the road following him around. They were there while he was preaching and healing, as part of his group of followers. He was teaching them too, as well as his male disciples.

A group of women accompanying a young unmarried man around Galilee, on a journey up to Jerusalem, and tagging along with his rag-tag band of followers in the Holy City, would undoubtedly have generated hostile comments and indecent rumours, generating a level of outrage among the fervent Jewish onlookers and in the ranks of the scribbling classes and among the Pharisees. He was already attracting attention – a friend of tax collectors and sinners; supposedly working his magic under the spell of the prince of devils, Beelzebub; eating and drinking with all kinds of people, at times with the riff-raff of the earth; ignoring proper etiquette and regulations. His association with unaccompanied female followers would only have added to his reputation as a dangerous rebel, generating scandal, intent on undermining the fabric of Jewish society.

As a rule, Jewish religious rabbis in Palestine in and around the first century did not enrol women as students in their classes, or allow them to associate with their male pupils, with their disciples. It seems unnecessary to add that, as a rule, married or even single women would not travel around the countryside alone, in the company of a rabbi of any persuasion. As authoritative interpreters of the Law, the sages did not contemplate the possibility that men and women would, or could, study the Torah together, in one another's company. In those days, in that culture, men and women were separated in ways unfamiliar and unacceptable to a modern Western man or woman.

The casual Jewish observer standing on a street corner, watching Jesus as he passed by, would have been amazed, perhaps even scandalised, to see a band of women as part of his entourage. And those early Jewish Christians listening attentively to the recollections of Peter and the Twelve, and to the other preachers, then later reading about Jesus in the Gospels of Mark or Matthew, would also have been shocked (or perhaps thrilled), to hear about Jesus and his female friends. The Greco-Roman readers of the Gospel of Luke would have been equally surprised. Rich women of the period might have felt free to offer some material support to a rabbi and his disciples, but for them to leave home and husband and to go on the road with a rambling rabbi – simply unheard of.

The documentary evidence available to us records that Jesus invited a number of his followers to be his disciples, to accompany him on his travels, to listen to him as he taught, to hear his message and attend the private sessions where he developed and explained the meaning hidden in his stories, to work wonders in his name and to go out into the villages and towns to prepare people for his arrival.

While the gospels recount a number of incidents where Jesus expressly invited some of the men who were now associated with him and listening to his message to be his disciples, there is no early documentary evidence to show that Jesus ever issued such an invitation to his female followers, either as a group or individually. 'Come, follow me' was not a command or invitation we hear addressed to Mary or Martha, or Joanna or any other woman. This does not mean, however, that during his public ministry, his female followers, or some of them, were not accepted by Jesus and others as his disciples. At the very least, the Jesus we meet in the gospels did not seek to dissuade them from joining his group. They were not, for example, sent about their business, back to their families. In fact, the gospels composers made it clear that he encouraged a number of women into his inner circle.

When the gospels were taking shape, however, maybe the material to be included in the final version was selected and tailored to establish the status and authority of Peter, of the Twelve, of the male disciples. Perhaps the gospel composers were more minded to provide the evidence to establish the authority of the male leaders within their communities. Perhaps tensions had developed between those men who were occupying positions of authority and some of the female members who believed they had a special gift (of prophecy, of teaching, of public praying, for example) and were seeking to assert their role within the community and had to be put back in their place. Every author had his riding instructions – a purpose, a plan that involved including some stories, excluding others. Obviously, not all the conversations, the sayings, the parables told, the wonders worked, the trips here and there, the encounters over a period of three years could possibly have been included in the written records.

So, we are challenged to seek in the documents available to us, in the Gospels such as they are, answers to two questions – did women follow Jesus on his travels? And if so, what was their role and were they considered his 'disciples'?

The Gospels clearly depict Jesus as being accompanied on his travels by female followers who ministered to him, who travelled with him from Galilee on the road to Jerusalem and who stood by him at his crucifixion when his male followers had deserted him.

Some scholars have concluded that the author of Luke was placing the group of women he refers to in Chapter 8 in the same close relationship to Jesus as the Twelve, and that the group called 'disciples' was a further distance away – and less important. It is not fanciful to suggest, as some scholars have done, that the three named women (Mary Magdalene, Joanna and Susannah) were meant by the author of Luke to parallel Jesus' inner circle of three men, his favourite companions (Peter, James and John). Scholars have observed that in Luke's Gospel the author was inclined to draw parallels between miracles, stories and parables – one parallel involving a male character, the other a female figure. Perhaps the three privileged male disciples were balanced against three specially chosen female followers.

During his public ministry, Jesus attracted crowds as he moved around, in and out of towns and villages. People off the streets and out of homes came to listen to him, to hear his stories and witness the wonders he was mysteriously able to perform. Some among the crowds, men and women, searched for him here and there and would follow his steps for a while. He had a reputation as a teacher and healer. These crowds gathered and dispersed. They listened and drifted off home.

But according to the authors of the gospels, Jesus was also attracting a semi-permanent group of men and women who would follow him around. From the ranks of these regular disciples, Jesus is said to have selected a special team of twelve to parallel the twelve Patriarchs of the Old Testament. The documents disclose that this inner group of twelve constituted Jesus' regular companions – all men. No women. Whether there were in fact twelve apostles, or whether the number is 'typological', reflecting the Old Testament Patriarchs has been a matter of some discussion and dispute, as we will see.

But at least we can say with some certainty that some of Jesus' semi-permanent followers were females. The author of Luke tells us that after his mission in and around Galilee, Jesus turned his face towards Jerusalem, beginning his long pilgrimage to the Temple city, to celebrate the Passover in the city of David, there to face allegations of treason and blasphemy resulting in a criminal conviction and execution. Women, many of them, were part of his circle of regular followers. He was sending messengers ahead, to make ready for his visits, going from village to village. He appointed seventy 'others' (or perhaps seventy-two) and sent them on, two by two, as an advance party, to every village and town he proposed to visit. He gave them instructions of what to do and how to behave: 'He who hears you hears me, and he who rejects you rejects me, and he who rejects me rejects him who sent me' (Luke10:16).

The seventy were given a mission to preach, and a power to work wonders in Jesus' name – authority over demons, power to step on serpents and scorpions without fear. Later, in the early church, women would be seen to exercise similar powers, at least for a short time – teaching, prophesying, serving and ministering. Bearing in mind the role women were playing in Jesus' public life and as witnesses of his resurrection appearances, it is not fanciful to suggest that some women were probably in the ranks of the followers commissioned to go ahead and prepare the way for Jesus.

Women were at every stage of the drama: women who had accompanied Jesus all the way from Galilee, women who were described in Luke's Gospel as among Jesus' established associates and steadfast followers. Women formed a visible and functioning cohort among those who were following Jesus. We might well be curious to know what they did each evening, after the sun had gone down. Though none of the gospel writers have ventured into that territory, it seems safe to assume at least that they sat around and talked – plotting and planning, reviewing the day's work. Where did Jesus and his band of male and female followers stay when they were on the road, visiting towns and villages? Under the stars? In hay sheds? Crammed into the local boarding house? A night or two sleeping on a rug in the corner of a friend's family room or in a shared room in the local boarding house. Many puzzling questions to ask, about meals, shopping, bathing, toilettes. We are left to our imagination for an answer.

In the minds of the gospel authors, women had undoubtedly been intimately involved in Jesus public life and were major players in the events of his death and resurrection. Whether this constituted them as 'disciples' would depend on what a disciple was and what he or she did. I'm inclined to conclude on the available evidence that women would have also been regarded, if not commissioned, by Jesus as his disciples.

CHAPTER NINE

Jesus' Close Encounters with the Opposite Sex

In addition to being presented by his theological biographers as a gifted storyteller, as a man who could teach with authority about a kingdom, as a wonder-worker, Jesus was also depicted as a rebel. An outrider. A disturber of peace and good order. A subversive figure prepared to take on the leaders of the establishment – the priests, the educated and the Pharisees. Rather than identifying with those in power, those with status and authority (as the institution does today in many parts of the world), Jesus swam upstream, against the tide, associating with foreigners, with lepers, contemptible tax collectors, sinners, the ritually impure, the blind and the lame, reprobates and fringe-dwellers – and with women. This was the edgy portrait which the four gospel composers, each on his own distinctive canvas, painted for their readers.

A Woman Caught in the Act

The Gospel of John, as we now have it, contains a story which didn't appear in the original manuscripts or in John's Gospel text until the third century – and a story which displays none of the characteristic features of the gospel author's literary style or theology.

Jesus was in the Temple early in the morning, teaching, as he is presented in the Gospel of Luke. For various reasons, this story probably belonged to the Lucan material circulating as part of the early Christian tradition and was uplifted at a later stage and incorporated into the Gospel of John. The story fits neatly after what Luke recorded.

> And every day he was teaching in the Temple, but at night he went out and bunkered down, just like a classical swagman, on the hill known as Olivet. Early in the morning all the people would come to the Temple to hear him.*

According to the story, the authorities were trying to entrap Jesus and tarnish his reputation as an influential spiritual leader. To advance their devilish plan, they sought advice from Jesus about how he would deal with some poor woman they had sprung in the act of sexual concourse with someone else's husband. This was their opportunity. They could kill two birds with the one stone – bludgeon the woman to death for adultery, and level a charge of religious disloyalty against the preacher from the bush. The lynch mob addressed Jesus by the same title Mary Magdalene would use when she finally recognised him in the Garden after the Resurrection,

'Teacher, this woman has been caught in the act of adultery. In the law Moses commanded us to stone her to death. What do you think we should do?'

The trap was set. Jesus was wedged in a no-win situation, or so the Jerusalem elite thought. But in the story he is not presented as a man troubled by this dilemma, as someone under the pump and careful not to scandalise, careful not to make a mistake. He was in control – demanding attention, surrounded by silence, standing above and beyond the crowd, as a figure emitting sparks of authority and about to do the unexpected. He was going to attempt something extraordinary – he was going to answer their question.

First, one might ask, where was the Adam in this sorry saga – the lust-filled gentleman? According to the Mosaic Law, given that the woman was married, both offenders were liable to be exposed and condemned to death. The law charged the man to refrain from desiring or possessing another man's house, his man- or maid-servant, his ox, his ass or his wife. According to the law, the responsibility for sexual restraint fell on the man – but the culprit was nowhere to be seen. The punishment was going to fall on the woman. She was being publicly exposed and humiliated, and condemned for the opprobrium she was unloading on her family. The offending male had skulked away with nothing to fear from the prosecutors. It seems that 'boys will be boys' was as potent an excuse at the time of Jesus as it is today. In a patriarchal society the men were in control. They had their hands on the levers of power.

The scribes and Pharisees were finally about to score a victory. If Jesus was inclined to follow the law and condemn the poor woman, subjecting her to the harsh and heartless, but perfectly proper treatment under the law, the Roman authorities would descend on him for his part in an unauthorised execution. At that particular time in the history of Palestine, executions were reserved exclusively to the invading forces.

But he was not fazed. According to the story, cool as a cucumber, Jesus bent over and traced (perhaps wrote), something in the ground. While it was against the law to scribble or write even as few as two letters on the Sabbath, writing a few words in the dust seems to have been viewed more leniently.

Jesus was not famous for abiding by the details of the law, but on this occasion, perhaps a little amused, with a smile crossing his face, he shocked the academics and Pharisees with his knowing conformity. We have no idea what he wrote. Apparently something significant, something powerful, perhaps something embarrassing – or perhaps nothing, only some disconcerting doodle.

Why aren't we told? That message in the sand is precisely where our modern mind is focused, but we'll never know. His marks have long since been scattered on the wind. And if he was writing a brief note in the sand, this is the one and only occasion we know of when Jesus wrote. No file of speech-notes and interviews. No short stories or parables committed to writing. No collection of pithy sayings recorded in a notebook and kept in his pocket. No policy statement preserved for posterity on papyrus. Jesus was a man of action, and a man of his word – his spoken word.

Apparently, what Jesus did or said was enough to scatter the lynch mob that had gathered around the woman. He had said something about who had the right to cast the first deadly stone. Maybe they all realised that as men, they were largely responsible for the sexual crimes being committed in their towns and villages. Perhaps they had themselves played around. Slowly they all drifted away, leaving Jesus alone with the woman.

No death penalty for Jesus. No harsh condemnation. He wasn't a religious hard-liner. As far as he was concerned, the particular Law of Moses, even if it had come down from Heaven, was not going to be enforced. The world was destined to be governed by a new law. The power of God's unlimited mercy was to overwhelm Jesus' Kingdom of Heaven. Compassion. Acceptance of others, whoever they were – strangers, sinners, women.

Jesus stood there alone, a powerful figure in the company of this shaken creature and, contrary to the law, they spoke together, if only for a moment. Jesus shouldn't have been talking to her at all. She was a woman, a stranger, a sinner – and unclean to boot, from recent sexual contact. But he addressed her, and by the same title he used at Cana for his own mother – the same as he would repeat from the cross on Calvary. He looked at her tenderly, respectfully, affectionately, and said,

'Woman, where are they? Has no one condemned you?'

'No one, Lord,' she said.

The soft words that Jesus spoke next weren't heard by the mob of men who had wanted the death penalty, who had sought to wedge the Teacher into a legally compromising position. They had gone. Only the woman stood there in the open, exposed and shaking. She didn't need to be subjected to any more condemnation. She needed to be wrapped tight in arms of compassion.

And Jesus said, 'Neither do I condemn you; go, and sin no more.' (John 8:10-11)

Such a touching scene. Unworthy male accusers; a fragile female 'offender'. No double standard for him. He had come to set prisoners free, to claim the lost sheep. He couldn't condemn the woman, especially when the other party had disappeared into the crowd. No discrimination in the Kingdom of Heaven and a completely new code to replace the Old Law.

Jesus was triumphant again: a lay teacher in an illegal conversation with a woman. And in this relationship he was manifesting publicly the presence of the sacred to the world, there in the very heart of Jewish faith and practice.

The Foreign Woman at the Well

In his Gospel of John, the author penned an amusing account of Jesus' private encounter with a flighty Samaritan woman while his companions were away in town looking to buy food for weary members of the team and their leader. As the author presented it, it was just a casual meeting, half an hour or so of fame, and the woman never to be seen again. In the process, Jesus offended a number of taboos and rode roughshod over some important Jewish customs.

To avoid an inevitable confrontation with the establishment down south, Jesus was withdrawing back to his home turf in Galilee, taking the quick route through foreign, hostile territory, a journey of about three days according to Josephus. At midday, tired and thirsty, he sat down to rest near an ancient, well-established water source. Through a conversation with a Samaritan woman the author went on in his narrative to exploit the symbolism of this well and to develop a typological link between Jesus and Jacob – a popular literary device in the author's day, but one that fails to attract the attention of modern men and women. Modern readers seem to have lost their sense of places that are regarded as sacred, of their ancestors' fascination with history's links to the present.

Jesus was alone by the well when this woman appeared, unaccompanied and carrying an empty water jar. And contrary to the Jewish law, he initiated a conversation with her. Very strange. First, Jews and Samaritans, though distant blood cousins, couldn't stand one another – and two thousand years has still not softened their hearts. In those days, Jews dismissed Samaritans as heretics. They were engaged in idolatrous worship outside Jerusalem. If only for this reason, Jesus should not have been speaking to this woman, and she was aware that he was stepping over the mark, out of the square, ignoring the rules. Contact, any contact, was taboo.

Furthermore, Jesus asked to share the fresh cool water a filthy foreigner had drawn from the well of Jacob. He was willing to drink from a ritually impure vessel, the property of a ritually unclean woman – a heretic no less, and a sinner – and thereby, according to the law, he was ready to contaminate himself.

Thirdly, she was a woman. What did he think he was doing? When the disciples returned with food, naturally they 'were surprised to find him speaking to a woman'. But despite their surprise, their puzzlement, none of them was prepared to challenge him. He was beyond challenge, even by his close followers who were travelling with him. They were in awe of him. But they knew, and Jesus would have known, that a man was forbidden to converse in public with a woman, any woman, even his wife, and that a rabbi was prohibited from discussing theology with a member of the opposite sex. Jesus was openly ignoring the law – in fact, flouting the law. The situation was out of bounds on a number of levels.

And fourthly, as on other occasions, Jesus was happy to deal with a sinful woman. The woman who had been taken in adultery and whom he saved from a cruel death by scribbling something in the sand had been engaged in a brief conversation with Jesus and encouraged to go in peace with his blessing. This lady at the well of Jacob had had five husbands, and the man she was sleeping with at the time she met with Jesus was not one of those five. She was living on the fringe of the community, coming to draw water at the hottest time of the day, when none of the other women were there talking and gossiping. An outsider. Someone to avoid. A woman who could compromise a man's ritual purity and sully his reputation. But, as he was described by the Gospel writers, Jesus seemed to be attracted to these people, and they to him. A Jewish teacher should not have ventured into this forbidden territory.

There in the open, in public, under the blaze of the sun, by the well, Jesus and this woman had an extended conversation about deeply personal and spiritual matters. She was curious, and not the least shy. According to the author of the gospel, Jesus seized this opportunity to disclose profound insights about his life and mission, insights he had not yet shared with his companions, as far as we know. Here at the well, he began to share intimate secrets – with a foreigner, a woman, a social outcast.

The author presented his Master-Teacher as being completely open with a stranger – untroubled, honest, relaxed and uncomplicated in the presence of this multi-married, adulterous Samaritan. She questioned him, teased him, challenged him, and was eventually spellbound by what he had to say. Jesus did not play with this woman in the same way as he played with scribes and Pharisees. He treated her seriously. There was an immediate connection between the two of them. The conversation was raw, blunt. They went straight into it, hammer and tongs. No theological spin. Two adults conversing about serious issues.

Throughout the encounter, Jesus speaks with authority and radiates a mysterious presence. The woman is impressed. She is feisty and independent, with a sense of fun. Jesus is seen as persistent and penetrating. Sparks crackle off the conversation. Each deals with the other in a respectful manner. The dignity of Jesus and the dignity of the anonymous woman are preserved and shine through the narrative as they get right down to the existential substance of life and its meaning.

The story continued. After the encounter, the woman went back into town and proclaimed the message. She was the first preacher of the Good News we come across in John's Gospel and though we never meet her again, according to the text she was responsible for many people accepting the message of salvation that Jesus was preaching. Readers of the Bible will meet some Samaritan converts in the Acts of the Apostles. They just appear, out of nowhere. We have no idea where they had come from. Perhaps they had had the opportunity, some years before, to listen to the message of the woman Jesus had spoken to by the well of Jacob.

This woman with many husbands is an important figure in the story of the life of Jesus as told in John's Gospel. A Samaritan – no, a person; a woman, no, an individual who warranted respect. A sinner – no, an outsider, a stranger who was able to hear what Jesus was saying, someone who was free to respond to his vision. After a little conversation, she was fit for the kingdom.

This meeting by the well of Jacob at Shechem gives us a good idea how the early Johannine church thought of Jesus and how he related to others, to strangers, to women – happily, personally, intimately, respectfully, deeply.

Two Sisters at Home with Jesus

Martha and Mary lived with their brother Lazarus in a small town three kilometres east of Jerusalem, in Bethany, and according to the authors of the gospels of Luke and John, Jesus used to stay there from time to time. They were his friends, though they did not seem to move around with him and his other friends, in and out of towns and villages, up and down the country. They were settled in a town close to the Temple city and whenever Jesus travelled down to Jerusalem, he used to visit them.

The authors of the gospels did not think to tell us much about these three siblings and, like so many of the characters referred to in the sacred literature, they make a brief appearance and disappear off the scene, never to be heard of again. No reference in The Acts of the Apostles – a theological history which was composed by the author of Luke's Gospel and which traces the story of the establishment of the early Christian communities. Not even a whisper of them in the letters of Paul. Nothing. A puzzling silence, especially considering the close friendship these three enjoyed with the Teacher and the fantastic feat of raising Lazarus from the tomb.

We don't know how Jesus came to meet this family. Had Lazarus first met Jesus and then later, introduced the Preacher to his two sisters? Had Lazarus heard Jesus preaching and invited him home for a meal, and perhaps later, after they got to know him better, Lazarus asked him to stay with him and his sisters? Or had the sisters, or one of them, first heard Jesus delivering his message or seen him work a wonder, and from there, a special relationship had developed? We'll never know.

We don't know how Jesus came to be so close, so intimate with Lazarus and his sisters, or whether they were just some of the many friends whose company he enjoyed, whose hospitality he accepted. We have no idea where Jesus lived, or with whom. Perhaps he had rented a little hideaway somewhere, a place to call his own, where he could relax, cook a meal, have an afternoon nap, do his washing and hang it out in the sun, and entertain his followers. Maybe he boarded with friends – a bed somewhere out the back and money in an envelope to help defray the expenses. He had a reputation for being on the move, from village to village, across the country, and at least on occasions 'without a place to lay his head'.

We are not told whether any of the three siblings were married. No mention of a wife or a husband, or, for that matter, parents. Were they living alone? And if so, why? We don't know. And we don't know how old they were. We can imagine they were about the same age as Jesus, or maybe younger if they weren't married. Jesus seems to have been surrounded by a disproportionate number of men who were either not married or strangely free to spend time away from home.

Lazarus and his sisters seem to have been quite wealthy, if not rich, as they were able, according to the story, to put on a good party and provide an expensive, perfumed pot of nard to anoint their friend. Law-abiding Jews? Probably. The three of them seemed to be part of the Jewish community in the area – an inference available from the presence of those who had come down from Jerusalem to mourn with the sisters after Lazarus's death. Educated? Able to read and write? Who knows? No wonder later generations used their imagination to embellish these stories.

In several places in the gospels, we meet these two young women and their brother, as they grew to be important figures in Jesus' life. He loved to visit them in Bethany, to share meals with them, talk with them and relax in their company. As the authors of Luke and John would have us believe, the two sisters loved

Jesus, each in their own way. Both felt at home in his company, free to complain to him, free to ask a special favour.

Luke's author tells the story of Jesus answering a lawyer's question 'Who is my neighbour?' by recounting the parable of the Good Samaritan. Then, as 'they' (presumably Jesus and his disciples) went on their way, Jesus entered the 'village' and Martha invited him home. While she was much distracted fussing over the visitor, her sister Mary was sitting at his feet, an attentive student listening to the rabbi's teaching. Martha complained. She needed help in the kitchen and she saw her sister just lazing about.

> Martha, Martha, you are anxious and troubled about many things; one thing is important. Your sister has chosen the good portion of the arrangement between you both, and it will not be taken away from her.*

It is safe to conclude that as far as Jesus was concerned, if this story is true, a woman's role in society should not be limited to the kitchen – and the faith members of the early church agreed. They preserved the story and reported it. While society saw it as a woman's role to bear children, to suckle them and to keep house and please her husband, her real dignity, like that of any man, was based on her ability to respond to Jesus' message and to become part of the kingdom he was preaching. Mary had made the better choice. She was listening and attending while Martha was busy about other things.

In composing his gospel, the author of Luke was at pains to portray Jesus as a teacher. He taught in the synagogues of Galilee, and at Capernaum on the Sabbath: 'And they were astonished at his teaching, for his word had authority'(Luke 4:32).

Or as the Jerusalem Bible translated the statement: 'And his teaching made a deep impression on them because he spoke with authority.'

He was unusual. A lay teacher – self-taught – a classic autodidact. And unlike other teachers from the schools and synagogues, or those who were travelling around from place to place, this one could speak with clear authority. And he was a controversial rabbi, encouraging a woman to sit at his feet like male disciples, to share religious truths and explore spiritual experiences. The author of Luke was telling the story to let the community know that Jesus had encouraged a new role for women; if that wasn't the author's intention, that was the end result.

As a rule, the traditional roles for women involved giving birth to children, especially sons, working in the kitchen, cooking and serving, as Martha was busy doing. Jesus was breaking with the traditional role-playing. On another occasion, in the middle of a session of preaching, a woman in the crowd had raised her voice in praise of Jesus and his mother: 'Blessed is the womb that bore you, and the breasts that suckled you.' But however pleased he might have been with his mother being lauded, Jesus' response was swift and sharp: 'Blessed rather are those who hear the word of God and keep it.'

Jesus bypassed the ephemeral and went straight to the centre of human existence.

A woman's worth was not founded on her ability to bear children, but on her openness to God's word. A mother is a human being like her husband, a child of God and the equal of any man. She is not limited, as the Jewish social norms would have it, to womb-work or to housework. She too can be a student of the Torah and sit at the feet of any rabbi.

Luke's Gospel story is just another example of the same mentality. The author was inviting the community of believers to see Jesus encouraging his friend Mary to assume another role, one traditionally reserved to young Jewish men – learning at the feet of a teacher, engaging as a disciple of a rabbi, tuning into the word of God.

Jesus was at home, relaxed in mixed company, with female friends, doing what the Fathers of the Church – Jerome, Augustine,

John Chrysostom and many others – later would strongly advise against. He was fraternising with the enemy, taking no precautions to preserve his virginity, leaving himself open to the seductive wiles of women and the pernicious ways of the Evil One.

In his gospel, the author of John presented Jesus as someone his female friends could call on, as someone who loved their brother, who was moved to tears when confronted with his death, someone Mary could touch without embarrassment or condemnation. She felt free to anoint Jesus' body, free to deal with her male friend on an intimate, sensual level. Jesus was not a model for any seriously celibate clergyman. His early followers would have rules, strict rules to regulate fraternisation with females. For example, in 393 AD the Synod of Hippo decreed that

> The unmarried clergy of inferior orders may not visit virgins or widows without the permission of the bishops or priests, and even then not alone. Neither may bishops and priests visit such persons alone, but only in the company of clerics or worthy laymen.

But of course, though unmarried (a wife was never mentioned), Jesus was not a member of the inferior ranks of the clergy, or a bishop or priest. A mere layperson. Being Jewish, however, subject to the prescriptions of the law and bound by the cultural standards of the time, having female friendships was irregular, to say the least, and dangerous.

According to contemporary Jewish practices, as we have seen, women were not to be taught the Torah, or permitted to engage in serious theological conversation or in rabbinical studies. This is why the story recorded in Luke's Gospel, like the story of the Samaritan woman in John's, is so important. The authors were telling the members of his community that as far as Jesus was concerned, women were not excluded. They were free to enrol as students of theology because Jesus, during his public life, had changed the whole register. However other people outside the circle of the little Christian communities related to one another, women should be accepted as an active, visible part of the community life because they had been present at the centre of Jesus' life.

Picture the scene. A controversial, radical religious leader relaxing with friends. Two young women – one working in the kitchen, the other sitting close to Jesus, at his feet, listening to his teaching, questioning and conversing about life and spiritual issues. Just like his scribble in the sand, we have no idea what Jesus was saying to Mary, but his kingdom message is well known to us, set out in parables, in sayings and actions recorded in all four gospels. Something surprising, unconventional, intriguing, powerful, persuasive. About life and how we can please God, how to find salvation, something about a kingdom which is not of this world but which was among us. Love, selflessness. About a system of law scribbled on our hearts.

Mary was spellbound and her sister annoyed. Three good friends, at home in one another's company. In our society, men and women work together in the same office or factory, fight in the same military unit, boys and girls attend the same school and sit together in the same classes, the sexes mix and mingle freely at our universities. But in the cultural context of that time, Jesus' behaviour was unacceptable.

In addition to their appearance in Luke's Gospel, these three siblings from Bethany also make two appearances in John's Gospel.

The first passage is a long narrative recounting the fact of Lazarus' illness, his death, Jesus' late arrival in Bethany with his disciples, the sisters' insistent request that Jesus should do something special for them and Mary's spontaneous, naive declaration of faith.

The sisters had sent for Jesus with the message, 'Lord, he whom you love is ill'. Although particular friendships have been frowned on in monasteries and seminaries at least since the Middle Ages, by any standard, Lazarus and Jesus were special friends. For some unknown reason, according to the story, on receiving the message, Jesus delayed, but only two days, and in the face of danger to life and limb, he set out to return to Judaea – 'Jesus loved Martha and her sister, and Lazarus'.

As the story unfolded, Jesus already knew that Lazarus had passed away (we don't know how he had found out), but he had planned to return to the area where 'the Jews were by now seeking to stone' him, and Thomas, the doubting Twin, invited his fellow disciples to follow 'that we may die with him'. Serious stuff.

When Jesus arrived with his followers, outside the village, many Jewish folk from Jerusalem were already in Bethany to console the two sisters. These sisters were apparently part of the establishment and important in the area – or at least the author of John's Gospel wanted his readers to believe so. While Mary sat at home, her sister went to greet Jesus and gave him the news of their brother's death. In the story, he and Martha had a lengthy conversation about death and the resurrection, and Martha's outburst during this meeting appears as a full, spontaneous act of faith parallel to Peter's act of faith recorded by the author of Matthew in chapter 16:

> 'I am the resurrection and the life; he who believes in me, though he die, yet shall live, and whoever lives and believes in me shall never die. Do you believe this?' Martha said to him, 'Yes, Lord; I believe that you are the Christ, the Son of God, he who is coming into the world.' (John 11:25-27)

Jesus was looking for Martha's sister. Where was she? When Martha sent a message, Mary left the house quickly to meet Jesus. She threw herself at his feet, weeping and probably touching him, though even talking to this man in public would have been frowned upon.

'Lord, if you had been here, my brother would not have died'. Jesus was the healer, as well as the teacher. When he saw Mary weeping and the mourners following her, also weeping, he was deeply upset. He began to cry. He had lost a good friend, and the two sisters he was so close to were overcome at the loss of their beloved brother.

The remainder of this Johannine story, so laden with metaphorical motifs and theological material, is well known and does not need repeating at length. Lazarus was mysteriously restored to his family and the event caused some of the bystanders to believe, while others, seeking to cause trouble, reported the incident to the plotting Pharisees up in Jerusalem.

The Jewish priests and the Pharisees gathered in council to discuss their response and to plan an assassination – at least, this is the story John tells his readers, again infusing his theological subtext into the narrative.

What is astonishing is that, except for one brief reference, we never hear of Lazarus again. We don't know how much longer he lived, or where, or with whom, or what contribution he made to the life of the early community in and around Jerusalem, if any. Such an important person just disappeared.

The exceptional brief reference to Lazarus occurs at the beginning of chapter 12 of John's Gospel. The author wrote that before the Passover Jesus was in Bethany and a group of people (identified simply as 'they') got together to entertain him. 'They made him a supper' and Martha was serving the guests. Her brother, Lazarus, recently back from the dead, was among those at table with Jesus. This story was extremely important to the Christians of the early churches. It was recorded by the authors of all four Gospels – with some similarities and many puzzling variations. We should give these narratives closer attention.

A Female Admirer

According to the author of John's Gospel, Jesus was in Bethany at table with Lazarus and some others. Lazarus's sister, Martha, was busy serving them. Jesus' notoriety in the capital had increased and the opinion polls had turned ugly. The authorities were after him, looking for any opportunity to drag him off his pedestal. He had gone down to Bethany to be with friends. In the middle of the meal, Mary had taken a pound of costly ointment of pure nard, anointed Jesus' feet and wiped them with her hair. A rich, aromatic fragrance had wafted through the house.

One of the disciples, Judas Iscariot, the one who was going to betray his teacher, pretended to be offended by Mary's extravagance. He thought that the ointment should have been sold for three hundred denarii and the money distributed among the poor. What a pious hypocrite! He had been put in charge of the common money-purse and was exploiting his position to defraud his companions. Jesus was having none of Judas's deceitful generosity. Putting him back in his place, he said, 'Leave her alone. Get off her back. She will need this ointment to use on the day of my burial. The poor are always there with you, but I am not.'*

The meal came to an end. A crowd of Jews had learned that Jesus was there with Lazarus and since both had now become notorious, the mob had turned up to see them. Because of what had happened to Lazarus, many had left the synagogue and started to believe in Jesus, and as a result the chief priests had also planned to put Lazarus to the sword – or so the author wrote. If the facts are true, this may explain what happened to Lazarus, or at least why he might have gone to ground and disappeared off the scene.

The composer of John's Gospel was the only one of the four to set this extravagant anointing scene in Lazarus's house and to identify the weeping woman with his sister. The other three narratives set the stage in a different location, at a different time, and involve different characters. But we should follow the trail of the ointment, if only for a few steps further.

As far as can be seen, neither Martha nor her sister is mentioned as being present at Jesus' death. They are not mentioned by John as standing around on Calvary, or by Mark, and were probably not among 'his acquaintances and the women who had followed him from Galilee', who were standing at a distance watching the crucifixion, who had seen the tomb and how the body had been laid out, and who had prepared spices and ointments so they could go back to the tomb on the first day of the week to anoint the corpse. The sisters lived in Bethany, so they had not been among those women who had followed Jesus all the way from Galilee. It is just possible they were included among 'the many other women who had come up with him to Jerusalem'. So despite what Jesus is reported to have said to Judas at the meal in Bethany, the expensive pound of pure nard that Mary had used was probably not the ointment used on the day of his burial.

While it was the appropriate and traditional role of women to be involved in the intimate activity of preparing a body, male or female, for burial, anointing the body with oil and spices and wrapping it in linen, for a woman to feel free to offer sensual anointing services to a living male friend, for a man to accept such services without a polite protest, and in public, seems counter-intuitive and confronting. The relationship, as depicted by the Gospel writers and which Jesus enjoyed with his female friends and followers, was irregular, uncommonly sensual and intimate for that period.

The author of the original version of the story in the gospel attributed to Mark, had Jesus in Bethany, but only two days before the Passover (not six), and at the house of Simon the Leper – whoever he was. Perhaps the reader was supposed to know who he was, but how he came to be known by such an ignominious title is lost in the shadows of the ages. Maybe it was a playful nickname to capture some weird character trait of the host. Perhaps he had suffered from leprosy in past years and had recovered. Maybe the author wanted his readers to know that the host was himself unclean and that Jesus should not have been eating with him. Something else we'll never know.

As Jesus was sitting at table, eating and talking with Simon the Leper and other nameless men (only men), a woman appeared from stage left invading the gentlemen's private party and carrying an alabaster jar of ointment, dramatically smashed the jar and poured the contents over Jesus' head (not on his feet, as John's Gospel had alleged). Nothing about weeping and wiping. Some of those present were indignant and said among themselves (another variation) that the ointment was a waste and that it might have been sold for a good price, more than three hundred denarii (another slight variation), and given to the poor. The guests at the meal criticised the woman, but Jesus was on her side. He was more gracious, more generous towards the only woman in the room, apart, presumably, from the female slaves.

> Leave her alone. Why are you ruffling her feathers? She has done something truly beautiful for me. You always have the poor with you and whenever you want, you can do good to them [*another little difference*]. You won't always have me with you. She has done what she could. She has anointed my body for burial. Now, let me tell you that wherever the Gospel is preached in the whole world, what she has done today will be told in memory of her.*

That was how important this intimate service was considered by the early church. As long as the Gospel was preached, she would be remembered.

Mark's author finishes up with Judas Iscariot, one of the Twelve. He made an appointment with the chief priests to negotiate a deal to give up his boss for some paltry sum.

The author of Matthew's narrative followed the story of Mark's almost to the letter. Like Mark's version, the woman remained anonymous, but those who complained, according to Matthew's account, were the disciples; in lieu of the 300 denarii, they believed the ointment could have realised 'a large sum' on sale; and there is no mention of the group being at table. He also tailed his version with Judas Iscariot's meeting with the chief priests, adding that the offer was for thirty pieces of silver in exchange for delivering Jesus up.

As we have seen, John's author told the story of two women, both named, among a group of men including Lazarus and Jesus. The story in Mark and Matthew featured a single unnamed woman who interrupted a men's meeting which included Jesus, Simon the Leper, Judas Iscariot and the disciples.

The anointing story that the author of Luke recounted in his gospel is obviously a record based on the same incident, but one that the editor had worked and reworked so hard that it had taken on a life of its own. Jesus was not in Bethany with Lazarus and his sisters or with Simon the Leper, and it wasn't a few days before his death at Passover time. He had been preaching in the north, in and around Nain, early in his ministry. He had been invited to eat with Simon the Pharisee and his friends, at Simon's house. His host was a man of substance. He was a success in his small community and was paying the travelling prophet a considerable compliment by inviting him to dine with his friends. The men were at table enjoying themselves, discussing local affairs among themselves and with their guest when a woman of the street, a sinner, had learnt that Jesus was sitting at table in the Pharisee's home.

Reading between the lines, it seems Jesus had had previous contact with the woman in this story and had put her mind at ease by lifting a heavy burden of guilt from her heart, though at this distance we know nothing of her earlier life. So many things we'd like to know, but the author doesn't think to satisfy our curiosity. We're lucky to know as much as we do, though we must always bear in mind that the compiler has selected the material and put his slant on it. We see Jesus only as depicted by the author, and some decades after his death.

Some have suggested that in view of the limited employment opportunities available to women in those days, this faceless woman probably had been working on the streets. Whatever her occupation, she was certainly an outsider, contaminated in some way.

Most likely after a synagogue service, Jesus found himself eating at table with an important Pharisee. It is strange that we never hear of Jesus entertaining in his own home, on his own turf. In this story his host had welcomed him in a rather superior manner, without much fuss. Formal, but not warm. Willing to entertain, but not generous in his greeting. Aware of his dignity and superior status among his male friends. While Jesus, Simon and the other guests were relaxing at table, a woman of the city, a known sinner, carrying an alabaster flask of ointment, entered unannounced and made straight for one of Simon's guests. She stood behind Jesus, at his feet as he was reclining with the other faceless guests. Weeping, she began to moisten his feet with her cascading tears, to wipe them with her beautiful hair, to smother the Master's feet with kisses and anoint them with the expensive ointment she had brought to Simon's house just for that purpose. The host was far from pleased and began to think that Jesus was not the prophet he claimed to be. Otherwise he should have known the truth about this shameless sinner who was touching him. And Jesus had something to say to him – an unpleasant message to deliver to his host.

He told Simon the story of the two slaves whose debts had been cancelled by their master. Like one of these two men (the one whose master had written off the huge amount he owed), this woman had been relieved of a heavy load and as a consequence, she was deeply in love with him.

According to the story, Jesus was looking at the woman but speaking to his host, and in a surprisingly critical manner.

> Simon, do you see this woman? When I arrived at your home, you did not provide any water for me to wash my feet, but she has washed my feet with her tears and dried them with her hair. You did not greet me with a kiss, but from the time I entered your house, she has not ceased to kiss my feet. Are you getting the message? You treated me in a cavalier manner even though I was your guest, but she has more than made up for your rudeness. You did not anoint my head with oil, but she has anointed my feet with her ointment. Let me tell you, Simon, her sins, which are many, have been forgiven because she has loved much.
>
> Jesus continued to focus his attention on the woman. He said, 'Your faith has saved you. Go in peace.'*

Who was this mysterious female in Luke's story – the one with such faith, the woman with the glorious hair and the kissing lips, touching Jesus? Mary Magdalene? Perhaps. But Luke doesn't tell us, even though he knew Mary Magdalene by name. We'll never know. She must remain nameless.

In Mark's, Matthew's and John's gospels, the authors were using the story of this anointing to tell their readers that a woman had been intimately involved in preparing Jesus' body for burial, and letting them know how he had treated that woman with such delicate gracefulness.

The author of Luke's Gospel, however, used the story in a different way. He situated it in a completely different context at the beginning of Jesus' ministry, and drew a dramatic contrast between the snobbish behaviour of the strictly religious Pharisee who was the 'top dog' in his village, and the behaviour of a notorious woman who was possessed by a spirit of intense love for the wonder-working prophet. He compares the nameless woman whose sins had been forgiven with the fat, self-satisfied, judgmental Pharisee and his table-guests. The author used the story to teach his readers what response the Kingdom of Heaven expected of its citizens, and to paint a picture for his readers of Jesus at work, dealing with the religious right and a woman who was from the wrong side of the tracks and whom he permitted to minister to him in a particularly intimate manner – touching him, washing his feet, covering them with tears and kisses, shaking her beautiful long hair loose and allowing it to fall down over her face and shoulders in a most sensual, intimate manner. A gesture strictly forbidden for a Jewish woman with any sense of propriety – a provocation to any man with natural drives in his blood. A public scandal with Jesus at its centre. This encounter, which Luke's author narrated, and the incident at the well in Samaria, would be truly extraordinary stories in any era. They reveal in rainbow colours how relaxed Jesus was in the company of women, how he respected them, engaged with them, communicated on many levels with them, accepting without complication their personal, sometimes physical expressions of love and trust.

If the story is true, Jesus must have been somewhat surprised, and perhaps a little uncomfortable, as any man would be, to have become suddenly the centre of attention in another man's house, to have a woman, apparently known to all as a sinner, providing such a sensuous service exclusively for him, and in public. Her conduct was unseemly and extravagant. In such circumstances it might be difficult to maintain one's composure, to preserve one's dignity. Does one pretend that nothing is happening? Or politely distance oneself from the intruder? Politely refuse? Tuck your feet up under yourself on the couch? Or accept the attention graciously, without causing undue embarrassment to the over-exuberant, enthusiastic pedicurist?

In the story, this woman was paying Jesus a great compliment and showing no concern about what those who were present might think of her. Very irregular. The reader can tell from the tone of the narrative that Jesus had a great affection for her. The author wanted his readers to know what the community remembered about their fabulous Teacher. This relationship was more genuine, more profoundly personal, more intense and enriching than Jesus' relationship with his host, or with the other guests. Jesus must have been aware of what was going on around him, how they were thinking, how the others were reacting, but his attention was focused on the beautiful outsider at his feet and on the spontaneity, the generosity of her gift. This is the image of Jesus that Luke, and the other gospel writers, wanted their readers, the believers, to remember and cherish.

Noli me tangere was the command Jesus gave to his friend Mary Magdalene in the garden, immediately after his mysterious resurrection. 'Don't touch me' – and by way of explanation – because 'I have not yet ascended to the Father', claiming he was now changed into a spiritual being, living in another dimension, in another world.

But before his death, people could touch him, and often did. Women could touch him, even in a sensuous manner, and he would graciously welcome their attention. Not his wife, or his mother, or even his sisters. That might have been acceptable in the Jewish culture of the time, albeit only in the privacy of a family home. But these were friends, girlfriends, strangers, women off the street.

We will eventually compare, in another place, Jesus' unconventional, countercultural lifestyle and his relationship with his female friends, followers and disciples, with the rigid, ascetical obsessions of people such as Jerome, Tertullian and numerous medieval canonists, theologians and religious poets. *The Imitation of Christ* warned all who set out to follow the way of Jesus:–

> Keep company with the humble and simple, with the devout and godly, and speak of those things which nurture religion. Do not be familiar with any woman but, in general, commend all good women to God. Desire to be familiar only with God and with his angels and shun the acquaintance of men. (Book 1, chapter 8)

The advice of spiritual directors, to young, virile, innocent men in the seminary, preparing for priesthood at about the same age as Jesus was during his public ministry, was essentially 'no touching': no holding hands, no kissing, no embracing, no eye contact. Custody of the eyes forever. Monks, clerics, bishops and priests, all male, are different. Not meant to associate with those of the opposite sex. Unlike Jesus of Nazareth, priests have been brainwashed to believe that they are somehow different – mysteriously transformed into spiritual creatures, occupying an elevated realm, living apart, on a metaphysical pedestal and untouchable. *Noli me tangere* is the policy and order specially addressed by those in clerical orders to women, even to their mothers and sisters. Safety first. You can't be too careful. They are dangerous, perhaps even evil, doing the devil's work. And Jesus weeps. He was only a layperson from the north.

The Syrophoenician Woman

The gospels' authors would have us believe that Jesus was used to dealing with feisty women – the woman who had been caught in the act of adultery, for example, the much married woman by the well of Jacob, and his dear friend Mary Magdalene – but his prickly encounter with a Syrophoenician woman gives us reason to pause and question whether he was as gracious to women and as gentlemanly as he often appeared to be or as the stories in Luke's and John's gospels would have us believe. This story was not reported by them. Mark and Matthew's gospel writers might have had a somewhat more nuanced view of Jesus' contact with women, or perhaps he was just having a bad day and this woman was annoying him. Or maybe in the minds of the Mark and Matthew authors, he was more assertive, more macho, less sensitive, more distant, certainly not the emasculated Sacred Heart of Jesus figure many of us grew up with.

Putting the two narratives of Mark and Matthew together (for each composer supplies varying details), Jesus had withdrawn to the district of Tyre and Sidon, to an area north and west of his territory around Galilee, to an area where he felt safe, where he could be anonymous, where he could be relaxed in the home he had gone to. We don't know who lived there, or how Jesus had come to know the occupant. Another gap in the narrative, but a friend living in an isolated area – an acquaintance living in foreign and hostile territory, or a contact someone had given him. Matthew tells us Jesus' disciples were with him, so there was not much chance of peace and quiet in the house. No space for prayer. As we will see, perhaps some of these disciples were women. He was escaping from the sweaty crush of the crowd, but the peace he was seeking didn't last long.

A Canaanite woman (*Matthew*), a pagan of Syrophoenician birth (*Mark*) recognised Jesus and appeared to disturb his tranquillity. His reputation had preceded him and she wanted him to expel the demon that had taken over her daughter. Given his reputation, not an unreasonable request!

It's hard to believe that this foreign mother addressed Jesus as 'Lord' and 'Son of David'. Given that the incident actually took place, the author was undoubtedly overlaying a theological gloss on his narrative. The mother had heard of Jesus, pushed her way in, fell down at his feet (from the many references in the gospels, it appears that Jesus' feet had some attraction for women!), and begged a favour. But Jesus did not answer her. His disciples were irritated. They were being inconvenienced and wanted to get her out of there: 'Give her what she wants and send her away. She's crying after us.'

Jesus observed that his mission from God was to the lost sheep of Palestine, the underbelly of his own people, and by implication, not to heretics or pagans like herself. 'Let the children first be fed. It is not right to take the children's bread and throw it to the dogs.'

That was pretty direct, but according to the story, the mother was sharp and fiery. She was not cowed. She pushed on. This mysterious man, with his power over demons, didn't frighten her. She had her tormented daughter to consider and this might have been her only chance. Mothers are like that. Women can be persistent, and persistence can be annoying. Jesus was not going to escape. In fact he was to tell a parable about the value of a woman being annoying, pestering an indifferent judge for something she wanted. And this feisty female would not let Jesus off the hook that easily.

'Lord, help me.'

'It is not fair to take the children's bread and throw it to the dogs.'

On the surface, and perhaps even down deep, Jesus' reply seems harsh and insensitive. Dismissive, insulting, unnecessarily patronising. 'Dogs': what was he thinking? Gentiles were generally referred to by Jews as 'dogs', but how could anyone say such a thing to a pleading mother in need?

Perhaps Jesus was assuming the prejudices of his fellow Jews in order to teach his disciples that Gentiles were to be included as hearers of his message. Pretending in order to make something of the encounter. Or perhaps the authors of the two gospels were sending messages to their readers that Jesus had also had a mission outside Palestine, to the world at large, to pagans. In any event, his response was not as brutal as it appears in English. The word used in the text really meant 'puppies'. Maybe Jesus was teasing this persistent woman, talking to her playfully, affectionately. We don't hear his tone or see the look on his face. The early Christians were obviously okay with the story. Perhaps Jesus was reading the woman's body language and ploughed on. A desperate mother begging for her daughter and fighting to convince Jesus that he should do something for her.

> 'Yes, Lord, yet even the puppies eat the crumbs that fall from their master's table.'

Good for her. What a great riposte. Even strangers and pagans need food and have the right to be at table, if only to gather up the scraps on the floor. Her daughter would be satisfied with the scraps falling from God's table. Jesus was now not dealing with a foreigner, or an enemy, or an intruder, but with a mother out to do the best by her daughter. She was not a wilting violet. A strong woman, not to be trifled with, or denied. And human suffering has no bounds. Pain and anxiety torture all of God's children, Jew or pagan, rich or poor. This is a great story to tell. Jesus' mission might have been to Palestine, but God's compassion must be available to the whole world.

Jesus was moved by her great faith, by her conviction that even Syrophoenicians can also eat at his table. Addressing her by the same title he used for his mother, and for his dear friend Mary Magdalene, Jesus let go a powerful word: 'Woman, you have great faith. Let your wish be granted.'

As the two authors would have us believe, the daughter was healed instantly. The mother went home and found her daughter resting in bed, the demon gone. We never hear from her again, though Jesus had engaged with her, an outsider, on an adult level, and again outside the prevailing norms of contemporary society. Not controlled by opinion polls or focus groups. No slogans. A real outsider of deep faith who is presented to the reader as a model of what faith and persistence can achieve – not like his disciples who were men 'of little faith'.

The Woman Ritually and Permanently Impure

In the push and shove of the crowd, Jesus had noticed that someone had touched the fringe of his garment and he had felt a surge of power pulsing from him. An anonymous woman who had been disabled for twelve years with an embarrassing dribble of blood, desperately seeking relief, had summoned her courage and dared to touch him, secretly, under cover of a crowd milling around, in the hope of some magic cure. She had exhausted her savings on physicians and she was deteriorating. The haemorrhages were growing worse. Life flowing out of her body. The doctors had proved useless. Alternative medical treatments had disappointed. Jesus was her last hope.

The ebb and flow of the crowd itself speaks loudly of Jesus' charismatic power to attract, but the fact that such a tentative, gentle approach amid the noise and turmoil of the street didn't go unnoticed, is perhaps even more significant. The faceless woman's ritual impurity had prevented her from participating in the religious life and ceremony of her community. In fact this 'dirty' little woman was contaminating Jesus by daring to touch him.

According to the story, the faceless lady was well rewarded for seizing this passing opportunity, ignoring the trite rules and trivial regulations and placing her confidence in Jesus. She must have known him, at least by reputation, and while in awe of him, she wasn't in fear of him. Her private, hesitant reaching-out had not escaped the Preacher.

'Who touched me?'

'Don't be stupid. How would you ever know? Look at the crowd, pushing and shoving, jockeying for advantage.'

'Who touched me? Someone did.'*

Jesus addressed the lady warmly, affectionately.

> And when the woman saw that she had been uncovered, she came to him trembling, and falling down before him declared in the presence of all the people why she had touched him, and how she had been immediately cured. 'Daughter, your faith has made you well; go in peace.' (Luke 8:47-48)*

What are the three gospel storytellers telling their readers about Jesus and those close to him? They were providing an example of the faith Jesus was inviting from his followers a simple, humble, confident faith such as the haemorrhaging woman had demonstrated. And they wanted their readers to know that Jesus had been a powerful, popular and attractive man, sensitive to those around him, especially to the underprivileged – and women on the fringe. He was a man for women – and in those days, they were hard to find.

The Might of Widows

Of the four gospel writers, the author of Luke stands out as the one who prioritised the presence of women in the public life of Jesus and explored his special ministry to them. He clearly wanted his readers to understand that when it came to women, Jesus did not behave in a typical, culturally determined, patriarchal manner.

He valued women, included them in his ministry, embraced and encouraged them. He was aware of their dignity and importance. No mention of Eve and all the nonsense that went with her as the agent of Satan.

Scholars have observed that the author of the Gospel of Luke adopted a particular way of organising his material. He tended to record the parables or the events involving Jesus in pairs, following a recognisable pattern. This basic artificial structure in the composition appears frequently throughout his gospel. The author compared and contrasted two stories or episodes in Jesus' life, one involving a man, the other, a woman. Equal billing for both sexes.

Furthermore, throughout his gospel, the author seems to be asserting that men tend to be critical, suspicious, ambitious, hesitant, unreliable and doubting, while women appeared open, accepting, passionate, ready to participate and to experience the full range of responses, from joy and ecstasy to sorrow and tragedy. The men in Jesus' life were slow to believe, reluctant to accept what they were experiencing. Questioning, frightened, dumbfounded, jockeying for positions in the kingdom. Women, by contrast, were open to the new experience of the kingdom and the risen Lord. What is remarkable is that the women of the Gospels are presented in an entirely favourable light. As far as we can tell from the Gospels, Jesus never condemned women. He often condemned men, even his male disciples, especially those in power, those who were exercising authority over others. Never women – maybe in part because they were powerless – no one except the salacious daughter of Herodias, of course, and her power was based on her ability to please the basic instincts of a powerful man.

Women weren't the source of temptation and the progenitors of sin in Jesus' world. They were not the cause of cosmic chaos and human tragedy. They weren't seen by him as seductresses, or as frivolous, lazy, empty-headed creatures – inferior, and condemned to invisibility within the community. As far as we know, he never told them (as Paul would do) that they had to be submissive to their husbands, or to keep quiet; to dress in a certain way, or make sure their hair was covered. They were not seen by him as objects in a world of men. He did not criticise them, or send them back to their homes, or turn his back on them. He showed them respect and compassion. He was interested in them and listened to them. We never hear him following the advice of the wisdom literature and warning men to be seriously careful of them.

As he strolled with his disciples in the Temple precincts in Jerusalem, was Jesus the only one who happened to notice an old widow making her small contribution to the religious coffers? Here was another old lady, like the woman who had touched Jesus in the crowd, who was a model of faith and generosity to all believers, who was able to show in secret a heroic level of trust in providence and to surrender all her worldly wealth. This invisible widow's private generosity would not be hidden behind the shadows of history, unnoticed. What William Wordsworth might have described as her 'little, nameless, unremembered acts of kindness and of love' which are the 'best portion of a good [woman's] life' would not be a trivial gesture lost forever.

This simple story told by Luke's author at the beginning of chapter 21 tells us about Jesus, about what registered on his radar, about how he assessed what people did, what value he placed on human behaviour, and his attitude to the little people who generally went unnoticed, faceless. Capitalism in reverse. No access unless one 'donates' a large sum. The widow had donated practically nothing of any value, only two copper coins.

> Truly I tell you, this poor widow has put in more than all of them; for they all contributed out of their abundance (*Oh! That they would!**), but she out of her poverty put in all the living that she had. (Luke 21:3-4)

As a young man, Jesus identified with widows, with those in society who mingle like ghosts among us. They had a special place in his heart and were often on his mind. They feature constantly in the Gospel of Luke.

> And in the hearing of all the people he said to his disciples, 'Beware of the scribes, who like to go about in long robes, who love salutations in the market places and the best seats in the synagogues and the places of honour at feasts, who devour widows' houses and for a pretence make long prayers. They will receive the greater condemnation.' (Luke 20:45-47)

Luke's author also recorded the remembered complimentary words of Jesus about the widow of Zarephath and his praise for the fearless insistent widow hassling a hard-hearted judge.

He tells us of Jesus' ministry to Peter's mother-in-law and of his gift to the widow of Nain.

> Soon afterwards he went to a city called Nain, and his disciples and a great crowd went with him. As he drew near to the gate of the city, behold, a man who had died was being carried out, the only son of his mother, and she was a widow; and a large crowd from the city was with her. And when the Lord saw her, he had compassion on her and said to her, 'Do not weep' ... And the young man sat up, and began to speak. And he gave him to his mother. (Luke 7:11-15)*

In Jesus' mind, widows and orphans were symbols of the poor of his Gospel and were therefore especially blessed in the kingdom. He had an eye for widows. They were to become important in the life of the early church, and often vested with considerable power. But that's another story.

Chaos in the Synagogue

The story used to be told in the early church (and again recorded in the Gospel of Luke) about Jesus teaching in one of the local synagogues – a visiting speaker on a special occasion. All eyes on this strange teacher; all ears tuned to his message: a captive audience under orders to attend the synagogue on the Sabbath and being entertained by a young preacher of renown. The ruler of the synagogue was preening himself. He had arranged an exciting Sabbath celebration for his mountain village.

While Jesus was speaking he had caught a glimpse of an old lady hiding among the female congregation down the back. She shouldn't have been there – out of place and ritually unclean. For the past eighteen years she had been cursed with 'a spirit of infirmity' and the villagers naturally regarded her as possessed by demons.

The Law forbade a woman like her from entering the Temple in Jerusalem and from attending her local synagogue on the Sabbath. Bent over and twisted like a mess of barbed wire, she was a *persona non grata* in any assembly engaged in public worship. No one could speak to her, and certainly not touch her (even accidentally) without consequences. The ruler of the synagogue had obviously not seen her – he was duty-bound to have her expelled. A reject in the village.

If he had been doing his job properly, as the teacher of the day, the man in the pulpit was supposed to confront the intruder and order her out of the assembly. At the very least, Jesus could have pretended he hadn't seen her. Of course he knew the law, and like any Jew, he was bound to abide by the regulations. It was beyond acceptable that she could be treated with respect. She was a nobody in the scheme of things – and worse. Spoilt fruit on the barrow of life, bruised and worthless, and fit only for the rubbish bin.

There in the synagogue, in front of everybody, Jesus stepped over the line, out of the playing field of institutional religion, and without the least hesitation, he did four things which were strictly forbidden – he recognised the woman; he spoke to her; he touched her, thereby making himself ritually unclean; and he cured her of her 'spirit of infirmity' on the Sabbath. Diabolical! Even so far from the centre of power in Jerusalem, he was among conservative country people – pious Jews living their lives in accordance with the laws of Moses.

All hell broke loose. The ruler was mightily offended. The God-given regulations governing the Sabbath had been flouted. This maverick teacher had worked a wonder on the Sabbath and he had the effrontery to justify his behaviour:

'Is there one of you who does not untie his ox or his donkey from the manger on the Sabbath and take it out for watering?'

This story let the early believers know what their teacher had thought of the rules and regulations surrounding ritual purity and the Sabbath, how common sense trumped regulations, how he was prepared to deal with rulers and officials – 'you hypocrites' – and how he treated invisible women – old, disabled women.

But this old lady had not been invisible to Jesus, shameful or unclean. She was not a nobody in his eyes or in the soft eyes of God. Jesus regarded her as a daughter of the nation's founding father. Any law that excluded her, any regulation that demeaned her, which blemished and blamed her, offended the dictates of common sense, contradicted acceptable practice and was obviously completely stupid even though those in charge would have the faithful believe the rules had come down from God.

According to the story, Jesus was challenging his contemporaries, and the Church was inviting the Jewish Christians in its communities to look on their small world with fresh eyes, to reinterpret how we relate to one another in the kingdom, to enter the realm of a new reality with new ideas, new values and attitudes, where, inter alia, women enjoy a pre-eminence, where they are not stigmatised or controlled by ridiculous rules and prohibitions. 'All his adversaries were put to shame; and all the people rejoiced at the glorious things that were done by him.'

When Thomas Aquinas raised the question whether women could ever be ordained as priests, he identified the central issue to be whether a female member of our species could radiate the pre-eminence required of priesthood. That was the nub of it. But women were inferior. They are naturally subject to men. Less intelligent. Weaker. Less wise. More easily led astray and inclined to concupiscence. A misbegotten male, as his hero Aristotle had concluded. Created as man's helper, but only for generation, not for higher pursuits. Not equal to men who are governed by reason and discretion. Only men can truly signify the eminence, the status, the dignity, the nobility required to minister as a priest. Women were excluded. Even if someone like a bishop were to attempt to ordain a woman and performed all the ceremonials and ritual associated with the sacrament, she still would be just a laywoman. The male sexual equipment is a necessarily prerequisite to guarantee the validity of priestly ordination. That is what gives a candidate his pre-eminence. It's difficult to imagine Jesus agreeing.

An Ambitious Mother

When the author of Mark's Gospel tells the story, James and his brother John, sons of Zebedee, make a direct approach to Jesus in their attempt to beat the other apostles to the prestigious positions within the kingdom, but the story takes on a richer texture when Matthew's author records the same encounter. Without comment, he places a mother between Jesus and the two brothers. She does the asking. Jesus deals with her and offers her a vision of his kingdom.

Zebedee had been the managing director and owner of a successful family business. Until Jesus appeared on the scene, he and his two sons were fishermen on the Lake of Galilee – boats, nets, baskets – a small family business with debts and overdrafts. Then this itinerant preacher appeared out of the hills, talking nonsense about a kingdom, and the boys downed their hooks and sinkers, rolled up their nets, left home and followed him, leaving their father and mother to run the family business.

Jesus had completely disrupted the future plans of the Zebedee clan. The patriarch and his wife had had a plan of succession. They naturally expected their eldest son to take over the business, to marry and produce offspring and, on his father's death, to support his mother and become the head of the extended family. He should have been around to find a suitable husband for his unmarried sisters, to produce a dowry for them, to assist his brothers to establish themselves in the village community. That was how families operated. Instead the first-born had been enticed away, on a whim, to do God knew what. Family honour had been besmirched. People were talking. Hurtful gossip had gone the rounds and Mr and Mrs Zebedee were not talking, or perhaps the master of the house had already died.

As the story goes, this annoying, itinerant preacher had gone from strength to strength, preaching in villages, mesmerising the crowds, working wonders and winning a reputation as a man who spoke with strange authority. He was talking about a kingdom to come. Obviously, he was intending to liberate his people from the power of the Roman invaders and to save them from further oppression. Otherwise, what was all that about? People were saying he was John the Baptist who had come back to life, or Elijah, a prophet come down from God. Perhaps he was the promised Messiah the whole nation had been waiting for, a second Moses to stir up God's people and to lead them away from the forces of pagan occupation to establish a kingdom of glory.

As the story unfolds in the Gospel of Matthew, Mrs Zebedee goes in search of her two wandering sons in some futile attempt to remedy the family fortunes. If her husband had died in the meantime, in the absence of her sons, the burden of promoting the family fortunes had landed in her lap. In normal circumstances the father of the family would have borne the responsibility of dealing with his sons, confronting the preacher, bringing them back out of the wilderness to some resemblance of sanity. But for some reason, Mr Zebedee plays no part in the story. Something had happened.

The mother was away from home, out in the public domain where any normal woman would feel out of place, but compelled to approach a preacher, perhaps a total stranger, a male, and to speak with him. This was a cause of great anxiety and contrary to good manners, but she had to do what she could.

Women like Mrs Zebedee were defined in society by their husbands, dead or alive. In his account of the incident, the author of Matthew's Gospel does not favour his reader with the mother's name. Her friends might have addressed her as Muriel, or Daphne, but we are not told her proper name. She is introduced as the wife of a businessman, the mother of two young men whose names we know – James and John. Women had no public face in Palestine when Jesus was on the move. Unknown outside the home except as an adjunct to their husbands or as some male's mother – wife of old man Zebedee, mother of his two sons. If she had been a widow, and without her boys, she would have been a nobody.

The later apocryphal writings would have us believe that the mother of the two disciples of Jesus was the Salome who is mentioned by name twice in the Gospel of Mark. A comparison of Mark 15:40 and Matthew 27:56 would seem to suggest that the mother of James and John was this Salome who was also a follower of Jesus. But the matter is far from settled.

We should bear in mind that the Gospels were never meant to be exact historical records of events and in any event, when it comes to historical detail, they are notoriously inaccurate. There was a woman called Salome who was a disciple of Jesus and who was associated with Mary Magdalene. She appears in the Gospel of Mark (15:40 and 16:1) and later in the apocryphal literature – in the *Gospel of Thomas* (Saying 61), for example, and the *Protevangelion of James* (Ch. XIV) which reports her as present at the birth of Jesus and the first witness to the virginity of his mother.

> "And the midwife went out from the cave, and Salome met her. And the midwife said to her, "Salome, Salome, I will tell you a most surprising thing, which I saw. A virgin has brought forth, which is a thing contrary to nature." To which Salome replied, "As the Lord my God lives, unless I receive particular proof of this matter, I will not believe that a virgin has brought forth."
>
> Then Salome went in and the midwife said, "Mary, show yourself, for a great controversy has arisen about you." And Salome tested her with her finger. But her hand was withered and she groaned bitterly and said, "Woe to me, because of my iniquity! For I have tempted the living God, and my hand is ready to drop off."

However, in the *Greek Gospel of the Egyptians*, when Salome asked Jesus how long death would continue to dominate the earth, he answered - "So long as women continue to produce offspring, for I have come to end the works of the female." To this strange remark, Salome replies, "Then I have done well in not giving birth to children."

It would appear from this early second century document that according to an early tradition, the Salome who had been a disciple of Jesus was in fact childless and clearly not the mother of James and John, the one petitioning Jesus to bestow status and privilege on her sons.

Like a slave, like a maid, we see this woman kneeling at Jesus' feet – which was the typical pose adopted by slaves approaching their master and by those who were seeking a favour of Jesus – the slave seeking time to pay his account (Matthew 18:26); the Canaanite woman in the district of Tyre and Sidon (Matthew 15:25); the leper begging to be whole again (Matthew 8:2); the ruler requesting Jesus to do something wondrous for his daughter (Matthew 9:18) – everyone on his/her knees before Jesus.

> "Then the mother of the sons of Zebedee came up to him, with her sons, and kneeling before him she asked him for something." (Matthew 20:20)

She knew her place. It would have been better if she were invisible, but kneeling was the next best thing. Humility, respect, submission. No use approaching this man on equal terms, face-to-face. She wanted something – a favour. Something for her boys. Something for the family. And she was prepared to beg, there in public, in the presence of her sons.

> 'What do you want? Tell me – what are you looking for?'

> 'I want you to order that these two sons of mine will be given status and power in your kingdom. They have made big sacrifices, and the family has suffered in their absence. They should be rewarded – we should be rewarded. You are obviously on the move and we are expecting great things from you. Don't forget my sons. I want you to command that they will both be somebody in your new world – one on your right hand, one on your left, in your glory.' *

In requesting Jesus to appoint her men to positions of power in his kingdom, Mrs Zebedee was looking to the future of her family, perhaps seeking to find a profitable place for the family's assets. It is significant that the father figure is absent from the storyline and that the nobody-mother is given centre stage. Throughout the Gospels, the patriarchal figure that was so pre-eminent in contemporary society was systematically painted out of the picture in a series of encounters involving Jesus and his companions.

Towards the end of his Gospel, the author of Matthew recorded an address that Jesus made to his disciples (presumably also including the women who had followed him up to Jerusalem) and to 'the crowds'. He was criticising the scribes and Pharisees for their blatant hypocrisy and their crass stupidity. He told his followers that they were not to assume the title of Rabbi; that they had only one teacher and that they were all equal as brothers; and that they were to call no one their father because they had only one father, and he was in heaven. No one was more powerful than anyone else in Jesus' community, in his kingdom. God was their Father. His followers had to be careful not to turn his movement into a patriarchal, authoritarian, hierarchical society. No head of the family; no superior teacher; no specially positioned male with power and authority, but all brothers and sisters together.

In another story with echoes of Mrs Zebedee's insurance claim, the author of Mark's Gospel tells of Peter confronting Jesus about his future and that of his companions. They had left everything to follow him, and Jesus recognised what sacrifices they had all made for him and for the Gospel. He even listed what they all might have left behind – home, brothers, sisters, mother, father, children and lands. He assured them that they would receive an immediate hundredfold down payment and, in the future, 'eternal life'. In describing the reward they could expect in return for their sacrifice, he repeated his earlier list – but omitting 'fathers' – houses, brothers, sisters, mothers, children and lands – and added an additional reward – 'persecutions'. No mention of fathers in his kingdom. In the kingdom, no one was going to exercise a domineering, patriarchal authority over his followers. No owners – no bosses or superiors – no father figures or overseers – no Holinesses, or Graces, or Lords, or Majesties: a new type of family

– one without any entrenched authority structure. Men reduced in status to ordinary members of the kingdom, with women and children elevated to the position of full membership. 'Many that are first will be last, and the last first.'

Earlier in Mark's Gospel, the author had Jesus at home, talking to 'the crowd'. Men and women were seated around him when a message was delivered that his mother and some of his relatives had arrived and were asking to see him. As we have earlier observed, Jesus' answer was mysterious. He enquired out loud, as though to himself, 'Who are my mother and my relatives?' Then he turned to the people who were in a circle around him, 'Here are my mother and my relatives! Whoever does the will of God is my brother, and sister, and mother.' (Mark 3:35)

Again, no mention of a father figure. Jesus belonged to a new family. Whoever was a member of the kingdom, whoever did God's will would be his brother and sister and mother.

A kingdom on earth made up of believers, all equal in rank and status, and without a father figure of authority. No one with special rights and privileges. No one with ownership rights over his wife and daughters. That's the way the Creator had planned his original production – men and women partners, Eve equal to Adam, two in one flesh – and now Jesus was inviting his community, his followers, to bring themselves into conformity with God's original plan.

The legal practitioners among the Jewish people had challenged Jesus to set his seal of approval on their law of divorce that indulged the whims of husbands and enslaved wives as their chattels. Under the law, husbands could repudiate their wives, often for trivial reasons, and leave them destitute, while wives had no right of redress against their offending husbands – and Moses' law had come to them from God, or so the pious Jewish people believed. One of the great benefits of a patriarchal society was that men were always on the top – a protected species. How was Jesus going to deal with this inequality? Was this arrangement really God's will? Could he really, in all honesty, allow the women to suffer?

Jesus explained that Moses had allowed a husband to divorce his wife because of men's hardness of heart, because of their stupidity and stubbornness. But it had not always been like that, and with Jesus, things were going to be different. In his Kingdom of Heaven on earth, there was going to be a new law, a completely new regime. All men and women would be equal, as God had planned. Husbands and wives were meant to live together in mutual love and respect, to enjoy a life of intimacy with one another. Jesus was taking the side of the victim, of the women, and abolishing the male privilege. Women were no longer to be inferior and submissive. They were not property to be disposed of at will.

The world Jesus was in the process of creating was not one that Mrs Zebedee had imagined for herself and her sons. This was a world no one had heard of. No patriarch, no teachers or rabbis, no fathers and no masters. No hypocrites like the scribes and Pharisees. No places of honour, or phylacteries and long fringes, no cringing salutations in the marketplace – a world in which there were loving mothers and siblings, and no fathers. A world where the last would be first.

The early church was retelling the story for a reason. Many listeners had misunderstood what Jesus had been about. He hadn't come to establish a new order to replace Rome or the emperor. No places of pre-eminence. No medals or orders of merit. No seats of authority, or titles, or honours. His kingdom was not of this world, and yet this kneeling woman was still intent on pleading for favours and privileges for her sons – one to be the majordomo and the other his assistant.

'You have no idea what it is you are asking. Are you able, do you suppose, to drink from the same cup as me, or to suffer the same baptism in blood that is my destiny?' Jesus was now talking to her sons. Of course they could. No problem. They would be by his side during the uprisings and when the kingdom was established. They would be fighting along with him. They would be there when victory was declared, when he came to set up his throne, triumphant over the invaders. No sacrifice was too much when the reward was so attractive.

'Anything. We are ready and able.'

As the story unfolds in Matthew's Gospel, Jesus took the trouble to explain. He did not ignore his young followers' ambitious mother, or worse, disrespect her, chastise her, call her ignorant, wooden, hard of heart, blind, deaf like the Pharisees – hearing, but not understanding. He had on other occasions levelled these verbal blows at the Jewish intelligentsia, and even at his own apostles. But on this occasion, Jesus took the trouble to deal with a mother's request. She only wanted the best for her boys and her family, but she had no idea what she was talking about. Jesus paid her the compliment of putting her in the picture and explaining why he was in no position to grant her request.

> My Father is in charge. It's his kingdom coming. His will must be done. My Father has all these matters in mind. It is not for me to decide who sits where, or who is worthy, who pulls strings or controls the keys. The decision to separate the weeds from the wheat or who gets to occupy the senior ranks in the kingdom is not mine to make. My Father is the one in charge. He will decide – and in his own good time.*

The patriarchal idea of pre-eminence and power, of status and leadership that was at the root of Mrs Zebedee's request, would not apply in the kingdom Jesus was seeking to establish, where slaves and Gentiles, even women could expect to be treated like kings and company directors, like judges and millionaires – like men.

What a disappointment! The woman had had high hopes for her sons. But at least Jesus had treated her with respect – someone important enough to deserve an explanation.

Both authors of Mark's and Matthew's gospels record what happened later, after Jesus had answered Mrs. Zebedee's request. The other ten were irritated and annoyed. Two of their ranks had tried to steal a march on them and extract a promise of preferment from the captain. How dare they? But Jesus was on top of it. He had to explain once more what the position was, what he was about, what they could expect if they stayed with him. He summoned them and said,

> Look, you people still have absolutely no idea, have you? You think I am the same as the Roman governor, as Pontius Pilate or any of that crowd? They lord it over the little people, ordering them about, telling them what to do and not to do, exercising their authority. Get that right out of your heads. If you are going to be part of this ship and want to be great, you will have to be the servant of others. The first among you will be the slaves. I haven't come here to be served, to lay down the law and demand allegiance, but to lay down my life for others. There'll be no glory, or riches or positions on offer. This new world will be a realm beyond your dreams, so forget about frills and funny hats, about titles and special treatment in restaurants. If that's what you want, you'd better go somewhere else. My kingdom is not of this world.*

I'm not sure the apostles or their successors ever got the message, but Mrs Zebedee probably did.

Contrast the hostility and aggression Jesus showed in his treatment of the clerks, the local intellectuals and Pharisees with the delicacy and gracefulness, the respect he showed towards women – to Mrs Zebedee, to all women – Jews and foreigners, sinners and those who were ritually impure. The same gentleness and attention he showed to those who were destined to inherit the kingdom – lepers, the blind, the disabled and marginalised.

The four gospel composers recorded for their readers'

edification a series of incidents in which they depicted Jesus encountering various women on the byways and sidetracks, in and out of towns and villages, around Palestine and on his way to the centre of institutional religious malpractice. In most of these incidents, the relationship is off-beat. Marginalised women – unmarried, sinful, childless, non-Jewish women, women possessed by demons, shameless women, physically afflicted women, servants or slaves, penniless widows. A woman caught in the act of adultery, a woman from whom Jesus had expelled seven demons, a Samaritan woman with several husbands, a foreign Syrophoenician woman, a ritually impure, haemorrhaging old lady, a prostitute, two apparently unmarried and childless sisters, a slave girl hanging around on the fringe at Jesus' trial.

Apart from Mrs Zebedee, who had a husband and at least two irresponsible sons, there are no typically Jewish women to be seen. No happily married women living at home, looking after their husbands and children. The Gospel authors clearly wanted their readers to remember the Jesus who had adopted the fly-blown sheep, who had bound up the wounds of the stranger on the road, people who were on the margins of society, mangy, homeless women begging in the street, the mentally ill, those in refugee camps, behind barbed-wire fences, shunned by the wealthy and the religious establishment.

Jesus' treatment of women and his attitude to them, as portrayed by the four gospels, but particularly by Luke, typified him. This was who he was. He had discovered a new way of looking at the world, and he wanted to teach other people to share and enjoy his new world view – looking beyond the structures, the rules and the trivia, to the substance, to the spiritual, to a deeper meaning to our existence, and despite the bishop's hesitation as to whether any of us can know what was in his mind, as far as Jesus was concerned, women were destined to be an essential part of his new world.

CHAPTER TEN

The Women of the Passion

According to the author of Mark's Gospel, while Jesus was at Bethany in the house of Simon the Leper, an unnamed woman had appeared out of nowhere, upsetting Judas, the company treasurer, with her expensive jar of aromatic oil (three hundred denarii!) and humiliating him with her extravagant generosity.

A little later the same gospel tells the story of another unnamed woman, a young slave girl at the bottom of the social heap, who stepped out of the crowd to confront the keeper of the keys of heaven while Jesus was being quizzed by the chief priests, the elders and intellectuals of the Jewish community. An abrasive, outspoken girl giving voice to the uncomfortable truth that Peter was also one of them, an associate of the prisoner. And Peter, like the apostles after the resurrection, refused to accept the reality of his life and calling, even though he had earlier publicly sworn his allegiance, his readiness to fight right in the frontline, shoulder to shoulder with his leader. A little busy-body slave girl, feeling free to breach the social conventions of the day, startled the old fisherman from Galilee and made him confront who he really was. She was the cock announcing his betrayal – a voice from nowhere, a kick in the guts, a man's conscience speaking from the shadows. The apostle, full of bluster, was winded and knocked to his knees by an insignificant female servant.

The composer of the same gospel goes on to record that the women who had followed Jesus while he was journeying and preaching in Galilee, those who had ministered to him – Mary Magdalene, Mary the mother of James the younger and Joses, and Salome – were together in a huddle near Calvary, looking on as the Roman soldiers carried out their orders. And there were present 'many other women' who had come up with Jesus to Jerusalem – a crowd of women, but no mention of Jesus' male followers.

The author of Matthew's Gospel tells a similar story.

> There were also many women there, looking on from afar, who had followed Jesus from Galilee, ministering to him – among them were Mary Magdalene, and Mary the mother of James and Joseph, and the mother of the sons of Zebedee. (Matt 27:55-56)

No male friends or disciples.

Sometime later, we read of Mary Magdalene and the other Mary sitting opposite the sepulchre, watching Joseph of Arimathaea. He was burying the bruised body of the Preacher in someone else's tomb and rolling a massive stone across the entrance.

Describing the same tragic event, the author of the Gospel of Luke provides more detail. As recorded, all Jesus' acquaintances and the women who had followed him from Galilee stood at a distance and were eyewitnesses to the crucifixion. Unlike the others, Luke's author made no mention by name of any particular women. And again no mention of male supporters, though maybe there were some among 'the acquaintances'.

The Roman authorities entrusted Jesus' twisted corpse to a leading Pharisee, Joseph of Arimathea. The women followed him, saw the borrowed tomb and observed that the body of their teacher was being buried without any proper embalming. They went away to prepare spices and ointments, rested on the Sabbath and returned to the tomb on the first day of the week, early in the morning.

The Gospel of John makes no mention of the 'many women', or of any particular women who had followed Jesus from the north, but the author does identify a small group of four women standing close by, this time at the foot of the cross – Jesus' mother, her sister, Mary the wife of Clopas (the mother of James of Alphaeus) and Mary Magdalene (so many Marys!), and the disciple whom Jesus loved – the one Christians have assumed was John the apostle-evangelist. Who knows? Tradition tends to fill the gaps with ever-expanding legends. But at least, according to John's author, one male friend had showed up.

While the Gospels of Mark, Matthew and Luke recalled that the female friends of Jesus were standing at a distance on Calvary, with no male friends in sight, the memory of the same tragic event, which was handed down in the Gospel of John, was surprisingly different. Mary, the mother of Jesus, was there at the foot of the cross with the disciple whom Jesus loved, and, according to the author, Jesus spoke to them from his cross.

Throughout his description of the Calvary event, the author regularly asserted that segments of the story – for example, the soldiers' decision not to rip Jesus' garments and his seamless tunic apart – demonstrated Jesus' destiny to fulfil the prophecies from the Old Testament, passages that the author went on to quote. The narrative of the Calvary scene in John's Gospel was meticulously designed as a piece of literature.

According to John, when Jesus saw his mother and the disciple whom he loved standing nearby, at the foot of the cross, he said to his mother, 'Woman, behold your son'. Then Jesus turned to his disciple and addressed him, 'Behold your mother'.

And the account concluded:

> And from that hour (*that is, the hour long awaited and which had now arrived*), the disciple took Jesus' mother to his own home. (John 19:27)

Hard to believe that a man nailed to a cross, exhausted, bruised and bleeding, could see anything or anyone amid the earthquake of his pain, could think to make arrangements for his mother's continuing care. John's Calvary narrative reads more like a story which was made up within the Johannine community and which eventually found its way into the Gospel composed within that church.

Given that the disciple whom Jesus loved was entrusted by Jesus with the care of his mother, and provided we accept that this person is the same as the John who gave his name to the fourth gospel (a matter much in dispute), it is surprising that Mary was not given more prominence in this Gospel. She appears in one other place, at the beginning of the Gospel, in the company of her son at a wedding feast close to their hometown.

In his lengthy analysis of the Cana event and his extensive footnotes in the second volume of his book *A Marginal Jew*, John P. Meier reflected on many troubling aspects of the narrative, and concluded (albeit somewhat reluctantly) that he could not find a nugget of historical fact in the Gospel account. All symbolic and theological – the whole passage created by the author, with no foundation in any identifiable oral tradition.

> When one adds these historical difficulties to the massive amount of Johannine literary and theological traits permeating the whole story, it is difficult to identify any 'historical kernel' or 'core event' that might have a claim to go back to the historical Jesus. Put another way: if we subtract from the eleven verses of the first Cana miracle every element that is likely to have come from the creative mind of John or his Johannine 'school' and every element that raises historical problems, the entire pericope (*a short, self-contained passage from a book or document – a sequence of sentences that forms one unit which is suitable for public reading in a liturgical context**) vanishes before our eyes verse by verse. (p. 949)

However, the early Johannine community clearly wanted to record a story to establish the status and significance of Jesus' mother. In two passages, one at the beginning of the Gospel, the other at the end, Mary appears with her son and he addresses her by the special title of 'Woman' - a title which probably carried echoes of the first woman as she appeared in Genesis 3:15 and 20, Eve, the mythical mother of humanity. The author of the fourth Gospel, whoever he was, probably wanted his readers to accept Mary, the mother of Jesus and the adopted mother of the beloved disciple, as the true mother of all the citizens of the Kingdom of God, the first woman of the new creation established by Jesus. Echoes again of the central motif of Jesus' message, the kingdom.

However, we should not allow ourselves to be waylaid onto a byroad, however scenic. Our interest lies explicitly in what stories the early Christian communities told about Jesus and his contact with women, including, of course, his mother, about how women were presented in the canonical literature of the first century as part of Jesus' life.

Jesus' mother is never referred to by her proper name in the gospel written under the name of John. The other gospel writers all felt comfortable calling her 'Mary' and referring to other women by their first names, but the Johannine author steadfastly avoided naming Mary. He identified her as 'the mother of Jesus' (e.g. John 2:1, 3-5), and when Jesus is said to have addressed his mother, he referred to her as 'Woman', rather than 'Mother' or 'Mum'. With the sole exception of the Gospel of John, in no other biblical passage, in the Old or the New Testaments, where a son is addressing his biological mother, does he refer to her by the title 'Woman'. Yet the author places that title on Jesus' lips, also when he spoke to Mary Magdalene in the garden near the empty tomb, and to the Samaritan woman at the well. The title also appeared in the later addition to the fourth gospel when a copyist added the story of Jesus saving the woman caught in adultery from stoning. Jesus also addressed this lady as 'Woman'.

However we may be inclined to interpret the title today as a mode of address, 'Woman' was not a slight, or a sign of disrespect. There was, however, a degree a formality associated with it. Given that the author knew Mary's proper name and avoided using it, and given that he identified her by the more formal phrase 'the mother of Jesus' and that he presented Jesus as addressing his mother by the title 'Woman', it seems reasonable to conclude that the composer constructed his material in such a way as to develop some sort of symbolic relationship between Jesus and his mother, at the beginning of his Gospel and at its conclusion when Jesus' hour of glorification on the cross had struck. The title seems to take on a tone of respect and special dignity attributed to Mary, to Mary Magdalene, to the Samaritan woman and to the poor woman caught in the act of adultery.

In John 2:1-11, Jesus' mother is seen as instrumental in her son's first of seven wondrous signs which the author recorded as proof of the authenticity of Jesus' mission as the Messiah, as the new Moses come to repeat on a much-enhanced level the prodigies of the Exodus. Although she disappears entirely from the body of his Gospel, Mary is present at the beginning (and at the end), playing an important role. The author was presenting this woman as a central figure in her son's public ministry, at his death and as a continuing figure in the life of his community after his death.

The author of John's Gospel concluded his imaginary, theological Cana story by stating, very simply, that after the wedding feast, Jesus went down to Capernaum with his mother and his disciples, and that they stayed there only a matter of a few days. The memory of Mary preserved within the Johannine community seems to have included the fact that at least on some occasions, his mother accompanied Jesus on his wanderings along with his disciples. She disappears from sight, however, after her intervention on behalf of the bridegroom's family at Cana and reappears much later on Calvary. How she came to be in Jerusalem at the time of her son's death does not form part of the story but given that she was there on Calvary, she had probably followed him and his travelling band of companions (men and women) on their journey up to Jerusalem, maybe to celebrate the Passover with them, as she and Joseph used to do each year.

As we have already seen, the Mark, Matthew and Luke gospels contain a brief glimpse of a puzzling encounter between Jesus on the one hand, and his mother and his relations on the other. These passages preserved some tradition within the early church that at least from time to time, Jesus' mother and some of the members of his family had found themselves in the same vicinity and had crossed paths with Jesus and his followers. Perhaps they were following him around, listening to his message and witnessing his wonders. Maybe what Jesus had said was not a rebuff to his family members, including his mother, but a declaration that by her faith and her way of life, she too had become a citizen of the Kingdom of Heaven, a member of his new family of faith.

And finally on the subject of the Passion women, who were those women along the road as Jesus, crowned with thorns, made his way up the hill to Calvary? Along with a 'great multitude of the people', a rabble who were following him, as well as a Simon from the town of Cyrene who was helping to carry his heavy cross, these women just appear, out of nowhere, in the passion text (without any explanation), wailing and lamenting. Where did they come from? Who were they? How did they know Jesus? Did he know them? Admirers? Friends? Professional mourners? A Greek chorus from the author's literary background? Or merely a literary device? We are not told, and we'll never know.

Women again. Part of the drama. Strangers to Jesus but playing their part. Even in the midst of his intense suffering, and against the cultural standards of the period, the early Christians wanted to record that Jesus addressed them as 'daughters of Jerusalem' and spoke his message directly to them.

The women Jesus had addressed as 'Woman' were all people on the fringe of society – a Samaritan lady, Mary Magdalene from whom Jesus had driven seven devils, the woman caught in the act of an adulterous relationship, and his own mother who at one stage, early in her life, had been found to be surprisingly and inconveniently pregnant – all social rejects but all kingdom people. Jesus was not mixing in the upper levels of society, but the women he was meeting were all treated respectfully.

CHAPTER ELEVEN

Any Women Around the Table of the Lord?

Given the fact that neither Paul of Tarsus nor any of the four gospel authors mention the presence of women at the last meal Jesus celebrated before his betrayal and death, and given that the gospels writers each record that Jesus' apostles were present on the occasion, perhaps I should simply answer the question whether there were women at the Last Supper with an unambiguous 'no' and get on with the rest of the story.

But it's not that simple. Over the centuries, church men have spun a vast library of theology and dogma from this one event in Jesus' life. At a very early stage in the life of the church, this last meal became a gathering of the utmost importance. It has provided the basis for the exclusion of women from the priesthood, from the papacy and from any significant position of power within the institution. Women were not there when it counted. They had not been welcomed into Jesus' inner circle – not part of his A-team of apostles.

Christians have presumed, for centuries, perhaps mistakenly, that the Last Supper, if it ever took place, was a men's-only affair – Jesus and his Twelve – like a meeting of old-boys from a private school.

This Last Supper was transformed into a pivotal event in the unfolding life of the Christian community after Jesus' disappearance. Theologians and ecclesiastical dogmatists have taught that it was at this event that Jesus instituted the central liturgical celebration for his new church – the Eucharist, the Mass.

According to them, he had transformed the Jewish Passover meal into the most significant sacral event in the life of his church – an event to be repeated over and over again, weekly, daily, in every little corner of the world, wherever Christians gathered in prayer or where a lonely priest found himself for the break of day.

According to them, his intention had been set in stone in that upper room – his priesthood was to be restricted to men. At this Jerusalem meal Jesus had ordained twelve men and commissioned them to do again, often, what he had done with broken bread and a cup of wine. He ordained men, not women, and for this reason, if for no other, the Church was forever obliged to exclude women from the ranks of its ministers. According to them, Jesus was clear on this point.

There have been other reasons put forward to keep women silent and under control – that their sister Eve was the first sinner and temptress, dangerous and perverse; that women suffered a natural inferiority; that men were by nature pre-eminent; that the sacred mysteries couldn't possibly, decently be conducted by those who were tainted by a monthly discharge of blood – but what happened at the meal Jesus held just before his death is the big one. Jesus showed his preference for men as his future ministers.

For this reason I propose to spend a little time reflecting on this Supper event. What happened on that night as it is described by Paul in one of his epistles and by the four gospel authors is absolutely critical for any Christian who insists on excluding women from the ranks, and equally, for those who would seek to involve them as 'feet-washers' in the kingdom.

The Supper event was treated in tantalisingly inadequate detail by all four gospel composers, and even more summarily a generation earlier, by Paul of Tarsus in his first epistle to the Christians living in Corinth – a daub of paint here, a streak of colour there, blanks, shadows, dreams, silences – studied abstraction to torment Christians down the centuries.

Given that John the apostle and son of Mrs Zebedee was the same person who later was associated with the Gospel of John (a question by no means yet resolved, though scholars tend to think they were different people), according to the records, only this John and Matthew the tax collector had been members of the original Twelve and therefore, at least according to the records, in a privileged position as eye-witnesses to record their personal recollections of the meal and its setting – who was present, what had occurred. It is a surprise, therefore, that the author of John did not think to describe any ceremony involving bread and wine to commemorate Jesus' broken body and blood poured out. His was the last written New Testament account of this supper and it doesn't include the narrative that later became so critical. Instead he records a strange encounter between Jesus and the apostle Peter in which Peter objected to Jesus attempting to wash his feet and Jesus informed him that in his world, they would all be living as Gentile slaves and washing other people's feet.

As we will see, though they never said so, perhaps Mark and maybe even Luke might have also been present at the meal that afternoon, somewhere in the background. And as for Paul, though his economic version of the event was the first in time, he was certainly not among the guests and had to rely on what had come down to him.

This pivotal event in the life of Jesus and the Church has been captured by many artists over the centuries. One only has to call to mind da Vinci's fresco painted in Italy at the end of the fifteenth century. This world-famous work provides a glimpse of a moment frozen in the course of the meal – the Master seated at the centre of a banquet table, his twelve apostles pressed together on each side of him, the places on the other side of the table, opposite Jesus, vacant. Bread and wine, glasses or goblets, pewter dishes, jugs of water, all carefully placed on a white, linen tablecloth frilled in lace. Da Vinci had modelled the setting, the furnishings and utensils on a typical refectory scene in a Dominican monastery in Italy. Jesus is depicted presiding at a type of Mass, his outstretched hands drawing attention to the Eucharistic bread and wine. A classical, but totally anachronistic snapshot which, over centuries of exposure, has been etched into our western subconscious – a Renaissance distortion of an event recorded by writers from the first century.

With all the baggage a modern Christian carries in his head, all the beliefs and prejudices, impressions and presumptions, it is difficult to look with fresh eyes at the New Testament narratives of the Last Supper – a meeting of friends, elevated by the forces of piety, ignorance, superstition and faith, into a supernatural realm beyond the reach of history.

The earliest source of what came to be known as 'the Last Supper' was dictated by Paul of Tarsus in the spring of 54 AD or thereabouts – twenty years or so after the event. He alone referred to the gathering as 'the Lord's Supper'. He was reprimanding members of the local community for a series of scandals which someone from Corinth had reported to him. From his letter we can conclude that the Christians in that cosmopolitan seaside city (and presumably elsewhere) used to meet in the home of one of the members of the community to share a communal meal. A practice had developed of coming together regularly, on the first day of the week, to pray, to reminisce with other believers and to eat together. It would seem that each person or family brought his own food and drink, and that contrary to the spirit of Jesus, there was not much sharing going on. No feet-washing; too much drinking; exclusion of others; separating into factions; women misbehaving, acting outrageously; some members eating too much with others sitting around with nothing on their plates. According to Paul, this was no way to celebrate the Lord's Supper at which, ideally, everyone, rich or poor, men and women, shared together the same meal – eating the same bread, drinking from the same cup and being in communion. It seems rather peculiar that an exclusively male meal had been converted so quickly into a general, rather chaotic assembly for all-comers, including women.

After Paul had had his say, telling the Corinthians what he thought of them, he went on to recount what he himself had been told about 'the Lord's Supper', about what we have come to accept as the Eucharistic community meal, the Mass. He had heard that on the night when he was betrayed, Jesus had taken bread, given thanks, broken the bread and had told those present that the blessed and broken bread was his body torn asunder for them. Then he had invited them to repeat what he had done 'in memory of me'.

After supper, 'in the same way', he had taken the cup (of wine), presumably again blessing it 'in the same way', and had told those present that the cup was a new covenant (a solemn alliance between God and his creation, between God and his people) sealed in his blood. Whenever they drank from a cup like this, Jesus had said, they were to drink 'in memory of me'. This ritual of broken bread and cup poured out, according to Paul, was a dramatic and symbolic proclamation of the death of Jesus – a ritual which had been handed down to him and which was reminiscent of the Jewish Passover and feast of Unleavened Bread.

Paul's account is short and to the point. No details. He does not, for example, tell us who was present, or when it took place, or where. But in addition to this early account of the Lord's Supper, there are three other later accounts, in the Gospels of Mark, Matthew and Luke, which fill in at least some of the gaps. They identify, for example, some of the individuals who were there (all males), and in addition, make mention, in generic terms, of others who were also present – 'the Twelve', for example, 'the apostles' and 'disciples'. These other three narratives move about, adding detail, sometimes divergent detail, to a basic storyline.

The Gospel of John does not provide much detail, and what detail there is (the washing of the feet, the date of the feast, the lengthy prayer of Jesus, the betrayal by Judas and Jesus' prolonged, one-sided conversations with his apostles before his death) does not coincide with the scant details provided by the other three – the location, the property owner, the water-carrier, furnishings, bread, wine, cups, the betrayal (one of the few common denominators), a number of brief conversations and the concluding detail that when 'they had sung a hymn', 'they' went out to the Mount of Olives.

Biblical scholars have exhausted themselves traipsing up and down, in and out of these brief Supper accounts – training their magnifying glasses on specks of detail, searching, digging, brushing, disputing and guessing. Some of them have concluded that these Last Supper passages are more like a liturgical text that had been preserved within the community and later inserted into the Gospel story – a liturgical text which was probably based on some event involving Jesus sharing a loaf of bread and a cup with his followers before his death – some kind of farewell occasion. According to these scholars, the account of what the community did liturgically, namely share bread and a cup in memory of Jesus, was later read back into the story of Jesus' final days. Consequently, a simple historical event has been clouded in uncertainty and overlaid with a liturgical text and theological interpretation. As a result, at this late stage, we cannot be certain of what Jesus did and said, though most agree that something did occur at a meal involving his followers – but who those followers were is the question which interests us here.

Although all four gospels agree that Jesus died on a Friday and that he had held a farewell meal on a Thursday evening, none of the early records of the event (and certainly none of the later records) state, or even suggest, that some women attended the farewell meal – Jesus' mother, for example, or Mary Magdalene, or the two sisters of Lazarus, or any of Jesus' other female friends, including the many women who had followed him from Galilee up to Jerusalem. According to four of the five early accounts (Paul was silent on the question of the attendees) the occasion was restricted to Jesus and his Twelve.

Whether an informed reader can go beyond what is positively stated in the records and establish at least the possibility of others sharing the meal, depends on a number of prior considerations, including (1) whether any meal in fact took place, or if the written records were only a literary device created by the authors to establish a basis for a later liturgical practice; (2) what type of meal it was that Jesus and his guests celebrated just before his death – an atypical Passover meal or some other quasi-liturgical meal or a simple get-together to say farewell; and (3) whether the accounts are basically historically correct, or so overlaid with a symbolic, theological topping that the details (bread and wine, the Twelve, the direction to repeat the ritual in memory of Jesus until he returned) cannot be confidently accepted as historically true.

In my opinion, given the level of detail dealing with the preparation of this gathering, and the description as to what had occurred in the upper room that afternoon and evening, and again the details of what happened afterwards (for example, the events in the Garden of Gethsemane), there can be little doubt that on the eve of his death, Jesus celebrated a farewell meal and that at least some of his specially chosen disciples were in attendance.

The authors of the gospels of Mark, Matthew and Luke described Jesus' farewell meal with his disciples as a type of Jewish Passover meal. They also reported that his death occurred on the very day of the Passover, namely, according to the Jewish calendar, on the 15th Nisan. According to John's Gospel, however, Jesus died on a different date, the 14th Nisan, being the Day of Preparation for the Passover and, as it turned out that year, the day before the Sabbath.

Because of the character of the documentary evidence, it is impossible from this distance to state with any confidence which version is right, and consequently, whether it was a Passover meal, or just an ordinary meal between friends, or a rather more formal farewell meal. We are too far away from the events of Jesus' death, and the documents too shadowy and conflicting. Both might be wrong. Both might be a gloss, for theological reasons, laid across a basic historical event.

Both the Passover and the feast of Unleavened Bread were occasions of pilgrimage – familial, communal feasts which involved all the members of a family or else members of a small Jewish community. Provided he or she was of the Jewish faith, no family member or close friend was excluded, and everyone present was expected to participate actively – men, women and children – without distinction. Jews from the outer villages and towns, men and women from far and near, would journey to the Temple in Jerusalem to celebrate together in the city of David.

As the records state, just before the Passover and the feast of Unleavened Bread, Jesus had come up to Jerusalem, all the way from Galilee in the north, accompanied by a contingent of his faithful followers. According to Matthew's Gospel, his disciples had been with him at Bethany in the house of Simon the Leper, just two days before the Passover, and three days before the feast of Unleavened Bread. Some of those who had come up from Galilee were women, and the same women, or some of them, would stand at a distance to witness Jesus being put to death. They had apparently kept an eye on the events involving Jesus as they unfolded.

He had arrived with a group that included his mother, some women known to us by name as well as a band of other, nameless women. All these followers, men and women, were Jews, and according to all four gospels, irrespective of what chronology is correct (if any), all were in the Holy City at the time of the

Passover and on the feast of Unleavened Bread. All bound by law to celebrate the feast.

The mother of Jesus and Mary Magdalene pre-eminent among them, Mary the mother of James and Salome, Joanna, the mother of James, 'the other women with them' and the women who had come with him from Galilee – according to the author of The Acts of the Apostles these same women and the apostles (now reduced to eleven) had remained in Jerusalem after Jesus' final disappearance and had gathered in an 'upper room', where the apostles joined in praying with 'the women and Mary the mother of Jesus, and his brethren'. This intermingling of the sexes was not really allowed. They and the others had been in the city for at least a week, probably more, and they had to have been staying somewhere.

We are not told where Jesus' mother and his companions were staying, or with whom, or whether they were spending time in Jesus' company – whether they were among those listening to him teaching in the Temple, for example. Were some of them eating with him? All of them would have had to eat several times each day – but where and with whom? What were the arrangements among them while they were on pilgrimage in Jerusalem? We don't know whether some, or all of them, had relatives or friends in the big city – people in whose company and home they could stay and with whom they could celebrate the Passover. Perhaps they had to book into the equivalent of a caravan park or a small private hotel.

In telling the story, all four authors were frugal in the details they were providing. Instead of being confronted with the colours and shapes of a Rembrandt portrait, or the fascinating and fanciful details of one of the Breughel family paintings, we are condemned to a tantalising, puzzling piece of modern expressionist art and challenged to fill in the gaps with our historical imagination and best guesses. We have to read between the lines, plot the subtexts in the narratives, examine the surrounding literature describing the culture in which Jesus and his followers lived, and content ourselves with inferences and probabilities. From this distance, the exercise is difficult when even the sources, such as they are, are contradictory.

So where did Mary the mother of Jesus stay? And where did she celebrate the Passover? And with whom? Mary Magdalene? And the other women who had come up to Jerusalem with Jesus on his pilgrim journey? Why were they not present in the large upper room with Jesus and his Twelve, just as they had been with the apostles, on a later occasion, in the upper room after Jesus had finally disappeared from their midst? Had they been with friends somewhere else in the city? Were these women involved in a separate farewell celebration with Jesus before his death?

Bearing in mind the ebb and flow of the many considerations which focus on the issue, we cannot tell whether Jesus' meal with his disciples before his death was a Jewish Passover meal adapted to incorporate a prelude rite to commemorate Jesus' death, or whether it was a pre-Passover meal, or merely a fellowship meal before his death. Each account, whether one of the three basic accounts or the Johannine or Pauline accounts, is coloured with heavy theological and perhaps liturgical overlays – sacrificial lamb, sacrificial blood, sacrificial death, liberation, escape, Passover, new covenant and a new beginning. We cannot tell, and scholars cannot decide, where the simple truth lies.

If Jesus died on the Day of Preparation, on the 14th Nisan when the Passover lambs were slaughtered in the Temple, and if he was present at a meal during which he bade farewell to his disciples, we would need to overlook a good deal of the details in the other three texts, accepting that it had some theological significance but no historical weight, and instead rely on the details in John's Gospel. The specific Christian details relating to blessed and broken bread, a blessed cup shared, and how those ritual actions related to Jesus' death (what came to be known as the Eucharist) do not appear in John's account of the supper. No institution of the Eucharist and no ordination of any ministers. According to that source, the meal which Jesus shared with his followers took place sometime before his death, 'before the feast of the Passover', but at a time when Jesus was fully aware that his death was imminent. John's author tells the story, in colourful detail. In a simple dramatic gesture he captures what Jesus' kingdom message was about, namely, service of others. About washing feet. About welcoming and including, about acceptance and giving – attending to others, humbly, without ostentation. A loud action parable.

If John's chronology is preferred and the supper was a solemn farewell meal with Jesus' close associates, there were certainly others, apart from the Twelve, to whom Jesus had to address his farewell wishes before his death – the ones who had accompanied him from Galilee, including a group of female followers who were fully aware of what was about to happen to their leader. They obviously had had their ear to the ground. They were on the spot, on Calvary, witnessing the tragedy of his death. Jesus surely would have had to include them in any plans to gather his disciples for a farewell meal.

If Jesus had celebrated a Passover meal in Jerusalem on that fateful night, just before his arrest for inciting rebellion, it is inconceivable, given the family dimension of the particular religious feast, that his mother, in the first place, was not present, and secondly, that in addition to some of his close male associates around the table, at least some of his close female friends weren't also invited guests.

There seems to be no good reason why Jesus would have restricted his guest-list to the Twelve. If the occasion was so exclusive and the guest-list so restricted, it would have been the only occasion recorded in Jesus' public life when the door was closed to others. The Lord's Supper became the prototype as to how the whole community, men and women, rich and poor, were to celebrate and participate in Jesus' death and share in his kingdom. From the beginning, the doors were open to all comers. The Lord's Supper itself should have set this tone of inclusion. The faithful in Corinth were in no doubt about the fact that all had to be present at the bread-and-wine thanksgiving memorial meal.

So why wasn't the full guest-list included as part of the minutes of the meeting? At the time the records were being composed, those in charge of the community needed to establish the role and authority of the apostles and their successors as a discrete and influential group within the early Christian community. As we have seen, maybe the early authors were intent on drawing the parallel between the old and the new Palestine, between the twelve patriarchs as the foundation of the Jewish nation and the twelve apostles as the basis of the new, Christian community or conglomeration of believers. Twelve was a symbolic number for the Jews so when the authors were composing the Gospels and injecting their theological colours into the narrative of Jesus' last days, one of the themes they sought to exploit was continuity with the past. The farewell meal, whatever form it took and however many were present, was later made to carry a heavy theological burden.

So after all that, what are we to conclude? Despite the Passover framework in which three of the Gospel authors presented their narrative of this event, maybe the Last Supper was just that – a final get-together, one of many meals Jesus had had with his friends and followers, with his apostles (however many there were), with some hangers-on and with his female followers – but as it happened, the last one.

If the occasion was a farewell supper, Jesus either had a few of them with different guests, or if this was the only one, he couldn't have gone ahead and excluded people important to him. Some women had followed him all the way up to Jerusalem. They were, like him, visitors in the holy city. Some of them would be with him on Calvary the next day or at least within a few days. Given the respect with which Jesus had treated women throughout his life, given how important they were in his life, given their presence near him at such an important time, it is beyond belief that he would exclude them from his final official meeting.

Whatever the Gospel authors say in their theologically charged narratives of the Last Supper, it is highly probable that in addition to his apostles, Jesus had arranged to invite others, including his mother and at least some of his female friends.

CHAPTER TWELVE

The Resurrection Narratives

The various narratives that deal with Jesus' appearances after the resurrection reveal what the early church writers chose to tell their readers of the important role women had played in Jesus' new life.

According to the author of Luke's Gospel, after Jesus had collapsed dead on the cross, the women from Calvary had followed Joseph of Arimathea (who was a member of the Jewish governing council and had claimed Jesus' corpse for burial), and when they had seen the tomb and observed how the body had been laid out, they had gone back to Jerusalem to prepare burial spices and ointments.

These women returned to the tomb on the Sunday and found the rock blocking the door of the tomb had been rolled away, the tomb empty and the body gone. They were frightened. Two men 'in dazzling apparel' appeared out of nowhere and delivered a resurrection message: 'Why do you seek the living among the dead? He is not here, but has risen' (Luke 24:5).

These women who had come up with Jesus from Galilee (Mary Magdalene, Joanna and Mary the mother of James 'and the other women', went and told the eleven apostles and 'all the rest' (whoever they were), what they had seen and heard. The apostles did not believe them – just an idle tale, women imagining things, delusional. A typical culturally-determined response. No mention, however, of these women having actually encountered the risen Jesus.

The author also described a post-resurrection appearance to two disciples (one called Cleophas, the other anonymous). On the road to Emmaus, on the Sunday after Jesus' death, someone had come up beside them and started walking along with them. As the story went, they did not recognise who this man was – at least until he had broken bread with them. They reported to this stranger that some women 'of our company' – women in their group – had amazed them with the story that they had seen an empty tomb and a vision of angels who had announced that the Jesus who had been crucified was alive. They told the stranger that some of the men had gone to the tomb to check out what they had heard and found the women were telling the truth, but that, like the women themselves, these men had not seen Jesus either.

Without realising it, these two disciples had been walking and talking to a risen Jesus. Once their eyes had been opened and they had recognised this strange presence of someone they used to know in the flesh, he had vanished. They returned to Jerusalem to tell the others what had happened. The eleven were there 'and those who were with them' (undoubtedly some of the women), and they had told the two disciples that Jesus had indeed risen and had appeared to Simon. But, assuming that the two companions on the road were male, and not female, the author makes no mention of any appearance to women.

According to this Lucan version, while they were talking, Jesus again appeared and 'stood among them'. They thought they were witnessing an apparition and they were startled and frightened. Jesus tried to put their minds at peace. He showed them his hands and feet (pierced from the crucifixion), assuring them that he was 'flesh and bones' and not a spirit. And they saw him eating a piece of broiled fish.

In the story, those present had been the two Emmaus disciples, the eleven apostles and 'those who were with them' – presumably also the women who had earlier visited the tomb.

Jesus then began to open their minds, or so went the story which the author was telling for the edification of the early believers. Jesus began to discuss the Scriptures and to relate the sacred literature to himself, to his suffering, death and resurrection. He told them that they were the witnesses to these events, that they should preach in his name to all nations, beginning in Jerusalem, and that they should stay in the city until they had been 'clothed with power from on high' – and we learn from The Acts of the Apostles that some of those who stayed in the city awaiting the 'clothing', were women.

The author concluded his Gospel with a brief reference to Jesus' disappearance. He had been carried up into Heaven. After those who had been present had worshipped Jesus, they had returned to Jerusalem and had been continually in the Temple, blessing God. Of course, why not? They were still members of the Jewish faith and something truly extraordinary had just happened. Again, no mention of any women, though it seems likely there were some present among those who were with the eleven.

The same author took up the story of Jesus' disappearance at the beginning of his Acts of the Apostles. He recorded that before Jesus had been 'taken up', he had given a direction 'to the apostles whom he had chosen' – though at the end of his Gospel, according to the text, this commandment had been delivered to a larger group, to the two Emmaus disciples, the eleven and to those who had been with them.

Acts goes on to record that after his death, Jesus had presented himself 'to them' (to the apostles) 'by many proofs', appearing to them for forty days (which was a literary device to indicate a long time) and speaking to them of the 'Kingdom of God', his dominant message. Again, no mention of his appearances to women, though in fact, according to the records, they too had witnessed at least some of the 'proofs' over the period of forty days.

In Acts, the author expanded his account of Jesus' disappearance. He began with the general observation, 'when they had come together', and he wrote that 'they' had asked Jesus their usual question which showed once again that 'they' had completely missed the point of Jesus' message: 'Lord, will you at this time restore the kingdom of Palestine?'

But Jesus avoided the question. He told them he didn't know what his Father had planned for the future, but that they were to be his witnesses in Jerusalem, in all Judea and Samaria, and to the end of the earth. After he had disappeared out of sight, two men stood near them in white robes (like the two men at the tomb in Luke's Gospel) and addressed them as 'Men of Galilee'.

Were these strange men speaking to the eleven apostles only and ignoring the others who were present there? Or were those present restricted to the eleven? If so, where were the others? Had Jesus been speaking only to the apostles, letting them know they were his witnesses, or had he been addressing a larger group? And did that group include women? We will never know for sure. But what is our best guess?

The author writes that 'they' returned to Jerusalem and went to the upper-room where they were staying. And he tells us who the 'they' were – he identified the eleven apostles, by name. So it seems, according to the author, that those present to witness Jesus' disappearance on the mountain were the eleven apostles only – no one else. But they were not the only ones who had experienced the many proofs of his presence during the forty days. They were not the only ones who had heard him speaking of the Kingdom of God and not the only ones who would become his witnesses to all corners of the world. Women were part of this team of witnesses and the names of most of the eleven, apart from Peter, James and John, would quickly drop out of the official church rollcall – absent from the diptychs for a number of centuries. In any event, the eleven returned to Jerusalem and went straight to 'the upper room where they were staying' and spent the time in prayer 'together with the women and Mary the mother of Jesus, and with his brethren'.

Mark's version of these post-resurrection events was written well before Luke's and was somewhat different. He limited to three the women who approached the tomb after the Sabbath – Mary Magdalene, Mary the mother of James, and Salome – worrying as they went along about who would (could) roll the 'very large stone' away from the entrance to the tomb. But they needn't have worried. Someone had done the job before they arrived. When they entered the tomb, they encountered only one 'young man' (not two). He was sitting (not standing) on the right side, dressed in a white robe. One would think that however fallible memory might be, the details of these post-resurrection experiences would have been etched on the minds of those involved.

These tomb visitors were amazed. Of course, who wouldn't be? The young man told them that Jesus had risen and gone before them, north to Galilee, where they would see him. He instructed them to tell Jesus' disciples and Peter that he had gone before them to Galilee and that they would see him there. The women had fled trembling, amazed, and they had said nothing to anyone. And the story suddenly ends there.

According to the author of Mark, these women had not followed their instructions. They had not spoken to the eleven to tell them what had happened, or that Jesus would be seen in Galilee. Maybe it was the author's intention to conclude on this ambivalent note. Or perhaps he never had the chance to finish his Gospel. A number of verses were most likely added to the original text of Mark's Gospel. This probably occurred in the second century by the hand of some anonymous copier who wanted to produce a more satisfactory ending – a summary of the stories of Jesus' appearances and ascension based primarily on the Gospels of Luke and John.

This second century ghost-writer (or glossographer) had added, without fanfare, that early on the Sunday Jesus had appeared to the woman from whom he had cast out seven demons, Mary Magdalene. She had gone and told 'those who had been with him' – probably those who had been with him on his public preaching ministry, presumably the apostles and undoubtedly some others who had also accompanied him. She told 'them' that Jesus was alive and that she had seen him. But they didn't believe her. She was not a credible witness, only a female.

The ghost-writer had also told the readers that after Jesus had appeared to Mary Magdalene, he had appeared 'in another form' to 'two of them' as they were walking in the country. They had gone back and told 'the rest'. This brief statement was clearly a summary of the incident the author of Luke had recounted in more detail towards the end of his Gospel.

In Luke's Gospel, neither of these two men on the road to Emmaus had been members of the apostolic college, of the eleven. Perhaps we can conclude with some safety that 'the rest' referred to by the second century writer was a group of believers that probably included the apostles as well as others. In any event, whereas in the post-Mark version, 'they' did not believe what they were being told, the story that was told in the Gospel of Luke was different. Before the two Emmaus disciples could speak, 'the eleven and those who were with them' had their own story to tell. Jesus had appeared to Simon, thereby confirming the story of his appearance on the road to Emmaus.

The author of Matthew's Gospel told similar stories, but again with different and sometimes clashing details. According to him, only Mary Magdalene and 'the other Mary' had gone to the tomb on the Sunday, and only to see it, not to anoint the body. One angel had descended from heaven, rolled back the stone at the entrance and sat on it. This heavenly messenger appeared like lightning and his clothing was white as snow. The guards at the tomb had trembled and fainted. The angel had told the two women that Jesus had risen and he instructed them to go quickly and tell the disciples that they would see Jesus in Galilee. The two Marys, 'with fear and great joy', left the scene quickly and were running to tell the disciples when they met Jesus on the way. He spoke to them. They touched him. They took hold of his feet and worshipped him.

The Greek verb the author of Matthew's Gospel used was *krateo*, meaning 'to take hold of', 'to get possession of', 'to hold fast and not to let go', 'to lay hands on someone in order to have power over him', 'to rule, or control, or have mastery over'. The women didn't just touch Jesus; they took hold of him and didn't want to let him go. They grabbed his feet and held tight. Jesus told them not to be afraid but to go and tell his 'brethren' (his brothers and sisters) to go to Galilee and that they would see him there, not in Jerusalem.

John's Gospel tells a different story again, but with some strikingly similar details – a story to which Mark's ghost-writer had eluded briefly. According to the Johannine account, Mary Magdalene came to the tomb alone, not in the company of other women as the authors of Mark, Matthew and Luke had reported. However, once she had seen that the stone at the door of the tomb had been moved and had reported to Peter and John that Jesus' body had been taken away, she said, 'And we do not know where they have laid him.'

The 'we' may indicate that she was in fact not alone, though the remainder of the narrative makes no mention of any other women. In the narrative, as it unfolds, Peter and John ran to the tomb and saw that it was empty, that the linen burial-cloths had been left behind – but no sign of Jesus. While they returned to where they were staying, Mary had delayed at the tomb. She was weeping. Looking into the tomb, she saw two angels (not two men, not one angel – two angels) in white, who asked her why she was crying. She told them that Jesus' body had been taken away and she didn't know where he had been laid. She saw a man standing nearby but failed to recognise that it was in fact Jesus. Curious. She had known Jesus for quite a long time. They were not just casual acquaintances, but close friends. Now she thought that this figure in front of her was the local gardener. The author seems to have been painting a picture for his reader of a man in a garden with a woman, a new Genesis scene replacing the old story of Adam and Eve naked and innocent in the Garden of Eden.

Even when Jesus spoke to his friend, she still had no idea who he was: 'Sir, if you have carried him away, tell me where you have laid him, and I will take him away.'

In reply to her enquiry, Jesus uttered the simple word 'Mary', and immediately Mary Magdalene recognised him as her 'Rabboni', her Teacher. He addressed her by her first name – the name by which he had known her in a previous life – and she responded warmly, affectionately, calling him 'my dearest Teacher'. What a wondrous revelation! Jesus back with her, returned from the dead, in the flesh – like old times.

Before she had come in contact with her Teacher, months before, perhaps years, she had been a woman completely out of her mind, in the process of being destroyed by seven demons. A broken woman tormented by nightmares and evil spirits. Jesus had rescued her. He had lifted her out of the shadows and given her a life, turned her into a real person who could love and be loved, who could feel her own value, experience beauty, hold someone's hand and smile again. Her heart beat faster in Jesus' presence. Her body was lighter. He was able to make her feel special. She had become used to being a participant in those intense, intimate encounters.

But despite what this unexpected garden meeting looked like, despite Mary's special attachment to her Teacher, the encounters could not continue as before. That world had ended. Jesus had been executed. Their relationship had changed radically.

> Jesus said to her, 'Do not hold onto me. Don't touch me, for I have not yet ascended to the Father; but go to my brethren and say to them, I am ascending to my Father and your Father, to my God and your God'. (John 20:17-18)*

The risen Jesus was entrusting his friend, his female pupil with a special mission – to go and inform his followers, the members of his team, that he was going up to heaven. She was to be his messenger, and as the Church expanded, the Gnostic-Christians of the second and third centuries would portray Mary of Magdala as the apostle who understood – the woman with the 'gnosis', the insights, the hidden knowledge, who had been specially authorised as the interpreter of Jesus' message.

But what was the meaning of Jesus' blunt direction in the garden after the resurrection that his friend should not touch him. *Noli me tangere?* as Jerome later translated it. Why was Jesus telling Mary to pull back and not to touch him?

Some have suggested that her failure to recognise Jesus was a sign of her momentary lapse of faith. She had suddenly become a stranger. The great interpreter of biblical texts, Jerome the scholar, thought so. But this woman was one of the great female believers, and Jesus had been handled before, as we have seen, by women. Perhaps since the resurrection Jesus had become like the Ark of the Covenant – too sacred to be touched, too powerful, too dangerous to go near. His body had become out of bounds. Touching holy things and holy people can be dangerous for believers. Holy objects radiate an invisible and ominous power. They can explode. Ordinary mortals must be careful when they approach them. They burn – like the bush in the desert. They command respect. They evoke fear.

Mary Magdalene had taken hold of him and wouldn't let him go. Clinging to him. Jesus had to tell her to stop. The Greek verb the author used was *hapto*, which meant 'to fasten onto something and to bind fast', "to engage with or fasten onto someone in a wrestling contest, body-to-body', 'to hang onto, lay hold of, touch, grasp' and by extension, the word could also mean 'to set fire to, to kindle'.

The author used the present tense of the imperative form, signaling that Mary Magdalene had already taken hold of Jesus, physically, and that Jesus was telling her to stop doing what she was doing. She was embracing him, showing her affection for her Teacher. But Jesus was telling his friend that she must not try to hold him back, to take possession of him because he was already launched on his journey to the Father. For this reason, she should not be familiar with him in the way she had been before. She had to look beyond his physical presence and discover a new reality.

Although as far as we know Jesus did not speak Greek, the Greek verb the author put on Jesus' lips to order Mary to stop touching him in the manner she was, was regularly used as a euphemism for sexual contact. Paul used the same word in his first letter to Corinth where he quoted from the letter he had received from his church there, seeking his advice: 'It is well for a man not to touch a woman' (1 Cor. 7:1).

The word *hapto* could carry an obvious sexual reference. Not just touching, but wrestling with a woman body-to-body, holding fast to her, setting her on fire.

The same verb, with the same implications, can be found in The Book of Genesis and in The Book of Proverbs, and was used, again with sexual connotations, by contemporaries of the Johannine author, by Philo in dealing with a husband touching his wife during her period of menstruation, and by Josephus recording an unsavoury incident involving the breathtaking beauty of Sarah, wife of Abraham, and an Egyptian king's desire to touch her in her private parts. The word often carried physical, sexual overtones, but not always.

As instructed, Mary Magdalene released her hold on Jesus and went off to tell the disciples that she had seen 'the Lord', and what he had said. Based on her experience, she was presented to the reader as Jesus' messenger to carry the resurrection news to Jesus' brothers and sisters, to be his first witness to what had occurred. This was obviously a huge honour.

In a comparatively brief period Mary Magdalene was to be transformed into a heroic, mythical figure. Within a few generations she would be known as 'the apostle of apostles' and stories would be told of her in the blossoming apocryphal gospel literature.

Across the four gospels there are significant inconsistencies in the various narratives dealing with the visits to the tomb and Jesus' first appearances on Easter Sunday. They cannot all be historically, factually true, though despite the inconsistencies, there is a fundamental core of consistent facts. Some short time after his death, the tomb was empty and Jesus was said to be alive. In mysterious circumstances, he had appeared to various people, sometimes alone, sometimes in a group. For some mysterious reason, he had been difficult to recognise. Even those who had known Jesus well had not immediately recognised him. Even when they thought they knew who he was, none of them had dared to ask who he was. Their eyes had been opened and they had identified him only after he had addressed them by name, or in the breaking of bread, or when he had shared a meal on the beach with them, or after they had seen his wounds. Although the door had been locked, he had appeared out of nowhere to a group of his followers who were together in a room. It was Jesus, but he was changed – transformed and, according to John's Gospel, untouchable. Now part of a different world. Here, but functioning in a parallel reality. He would appear mysteriously, out of the blue, and then he'd vanish again, inexplicably, and eventually he was gone and did not return. And it's by no means insignificant that his new identity was first experienced by women, or perhaps a woman.

The overall inconsistencies may be explained by the fact that the various authors were reliant on and editing earlier sources. The inconsistencies are puzzling and call for an explanation, if one can be found. We should approach the different narratives with care. The agreement, however, from one version to another, as to the basic facts recounted – the characters involved, for example, what was reported as being said, the experience of Jesus' mysterious presence after his crucifixion – is evidence that something powerful had occurred and that Jesus' female friends were right at the centre of it, playing a major role as the drama unfolded.

On the evidence of two of the gospels, Matthew and John, women were at the heart of the resurrection experience, searching Jesus out and recognising him in the shadows, witnessing to his presence among them, even as the author of Matthew recorded, touching him. From the beginning of Jesus' ministry and from the beginning of the Christian era, women were in the middle of the action.

Paul's earlier account of Jesus' post-resurrection appearances (which completely excluded any reference to women) creates a whole new set of problems. I will postpone looking more closely at this issue for another occasion. But what is truly puzzling is that none of the material recorded in the Gospels (all the material we have reviewed that deals with Jesus' contact with women and how he treated them, as well as the vast amount of other Gospel material, except for the Transfiguration event, which makes an appearance in The Second Letter of Peter [1:16ff]) – none of it makes an appearance in any of the earlier Christian documents – in the authentic letters of St Paul, for example. No miracles, no sayings, no characters, no infancy details. No mention of John the

Baptiser, or Mary, or Mary Magdalene, or Lazarus. The Gospel material stands alone, as if Paul had never seen or heard of any of the stories about Jesus and his life in Palestine. He was writing his letters before any of the Gospel writers put pen to paper, before any of them gathered material to tell the story of Jesus. On his own say-so, he had had contact with at least some of the other apostles who had shared time with Jesus on the road, but nothing of their reminiscences scored a mention in his writings. Perhaps Paul was in the process of moving on into another world.

Towards the end of his First Letter to the Corinthians, Paul told his readers that he was handing on to them what he himself had been told, the Gospel he had received – that Jesus had been buried, that he had risen on the third day and that he had appeared to a range of people,

> To Cephas, then to the Twelve [*it had to have been to the eleven*]. Then he appeared to more than five hundred brethren at one time, most of whom are still alive, though some have fallen asleep. Then he appeared to James, then to all the apostles. Last of all, as to one untimely born, he appeared also to me. (1 Cor. 15:3-8)

In the light of what we have seen of the post-resurrection appearances as set out in the gospels, Paul's record of what had been handed down to him is of a completely different order. However, we only need to observe here that of the many appearances he alludes to, not one woman was involved.

CHAPTER THIRTEEN

The Post-Resurrection Infancy Narratives

When the infancy stories were being told and re-told, passed on and passed down, and recorded on parchment, Jesus had already lived his public life. He had been crucified and, according to the records, his followers had already experienced his strange presence among them before he had left them to return to his Father. Communities of believers had been established in Palestine and throughout the Greco-Roman world. Leaders, teachers and prophets, led by Paul of Tarsus and others (Peter and Apollos for example), had begun their reflections on the significance of Jesus' life, describing who he was for them, theologising about him and the events surrounding him.

The theological-historical sources recorded a series of incidents in Jesus' life, in his earthly as well as in his resurrection life, and as we have seen, many of these incidents involved women. On one level, these passages reflect the recorded memory of what the early Christians sought to conserve of the many possible stories that could have been told – what had been handed down, what had been preserved within the communities as distinct from what had been passed over, forgotten or rejected. These passages purported to register for his followers a genuine record (embellished with a theological slant) of the words of Jesus, of his parables, his responses, his reactions to various situations, his attitudes to others, his life principles and values.

But there is another set of passages in two of the four Gospels, material which came into existence after the resurrection, after

Jesus' mysterious, shadowy appearances among his disciples, after the process of theologising about Jesus had been well underway. This is the material that addressed events in the life of the child Jesus, before he had become the mature, adult, public, ministering and reacting figure. These infancy narratives, which appear at the beginning of the Matthew and Luke gospels, focused on his childhood – his mother and father, the strange circumstances surrounding his conception and birth, and on his ancestors. These were stories which were told and retold in the early church – simple incidents heavily overlaid with symbolic and theological considerations which evoked figures and incidents from the Old Testament stories and which reflected the beliefs and mentality of the early believers.

While the infancy narratives do not tell us anything about Jesus' responses to women and nothing about his readiness to embrace them in his life and mission, or about his discovery of girls as a teenager and the confusion of adolescent sexuality, the material at the beginning of the two gospels invites us to see what the members of the early church wanted to preserve about Jesus' birth and early life, and about the pre-eminent role of women in God's plan involving him, the Jewish people, and eventually all humanity.

A Lifeline for Jesus

If we can abstract from the metaphysical prologue of John's Gospel, the composer of that gospel and the author of Mark both ignored Jesus' early childhood and his genealogical line. Only the authors of the Matthew and Luke gospels began their story of Jesus' life with a selection of infancy and early childhood stories, and both traced his genealogical line far back, supposedly to its source.

For modern readers, trained from primary school in the basic rules of historical research, it is disconcerting to observe that the two genealogies set out in the Gospels have practically nothing in common. Luke's Gospel author constructed Jesus' lineage back to Adam who could only have been, on any view of the facts, a mythical figure conceived in the shadows of some storyteller's imagination. The author of Matthew's Gospel, on the other hand, identified Abraham as the source of Jesus' forebears and most scholars consider that he had been a real, historical character.

What does this say about the historical accuracy of these genealogies, or for that matter, about the overall accuracy of the gospel literature? The writers of these four gospels were not historians as we have come to know them in modern times – striving painstakingly for a detailed, factually accurate description of any given event, but never actually achieving it. They were authors of a different type of literature. They recorded a memory of some basic pivotal event (an encounter, a work of wonder, a story told to illustrate a message, a teaching or preaching event, a supper, a death), an event that had been overlaid with symbolic and theological considerations, covered in poetic literary devices, visionary and apocalyptic material.

The author of Matthew's Gospel made no effort to craft a punchy opening sentence or two to entice his reader to move beyond his initial paragraphs and become engrossed in his book. He began his literary effort with a turgid list of dreary names, the forebears of Jesus back to Abraham – sure-fire turn-off for any modern reader.

But in centuries now forgotten, genealogies of this kind were *de rigueur*. The Semitic tribes loved them, and they seem to have made a strong comeback on television in recent years with *Who Do You Think You Are?* In the early church, readers wanted to know the origins of their heroes, to trace their lifelines, to uncover the background to the central character of the book they were reading. Matthew's author wanted his readers to know that Jesus was linked to David, the King of Palestine, and to Abraham, the father of the Jewish nation.

And sprinkled in among the names of the different men from whom, according to Matthew's Gospel, Jesus apparently traced his lineage, were the names of a number of disreputable characters and of five shady women, including his own mother.

Of course Jesus' family tree at the commencement of Matthew's Gospel includes a number of admirable figures - good, holy men (Abraham, Isaac, Asa, Jehoshaphat, Uzziah, Jotham, Hezekiah and Josiah, to give a few examples) - but it also identifies a surprising number of truly wicked men – liars, murderers, adulterers, worshippers of pagan idols as well as a few female prostitutes. There is also quite a few characters nominated about whom we know next to nothing.

Apart from the well-known characters whose misdeeds are familiar to Jews and Christians alike (Jacob who had stolen his brother's birthright; Judah who had conspired to sell his half-brother Joseph into slavery in Egypt and who entered into marriage with a Canaanite woman; and of course, King David who was a notorious adulterer and murderer), there is a line of truly wicked men to whom Jesus was related by blood – at least the author of the Matthew Gospel would have us believe that his bloodline was far from squeaky clean.

King Rehoboam is an example. His genealogy is set out in 2 Chron. 11:17-20. We are told he was the son of Solomon and his mother was one of the king's many wives, Naanah the Ammonitess. The Bible records simply state that he had done evil - "for he did not set his heart to seek the Lord" (2 Chron. 12:14). Under his rule, Judah had turned to ways of wickedness – male cult prostitution was rampant throughout the land, wars being waged, blood being spilt, and pagan religious objects (*asherin*) which were associated with the worship of the fertility goddess Asherah, the consort of Ba'al, were available (2 Chron. 12:1-16 and I Kings 14:25-31).

King Abijah, another one of Jesus' relatives, the son of King Rehoboam and the grandson of King Solomon, is another example. As the Bible tells us, he had walked in all the sins which his father had committed before him. His heart had been twisted and not wholly true to the Lord (1 Kings 15:3). His family ties and his wicked deed are recorded in 2 Chron. 13:1-22 and 1 Kings 15:1-8.

The reference in 1 Kings identifies Abijah's mother as Maacah, the daughter of Abishalom, whereas the reference in 1 Chronicles states that his mother's name was Micaiah, the daughter of Uriel of Gibeah. It's not clear from the records who his mother was, but it is clear from these and other entries in the historical documents of the Old Testament that the mothers of powerful male figures were also seen as important. The authors of the sacred records took care to document the male bloodline as well as the maternal ancestry of those who succeeded King David and who were to precede the King-Messiah Palestine was expecting.

If the man who put together Jesus' family tree is to be believed, there was a team of skeletons in Jesus' family closet - and one of them had had a famous mother-in-law. Jezebel was a Phoenician princess who had married King Ahab and who had introduced the worship of Ba'al and the pagan god's consort Asherah into the land of Judah. She had engaged in cruel, licentious rites associated with the worship of these pagan gods. She had used her position as queen consort to undermine the worship of Yahweh in Palestine and to kill off the prophets of God. In the end, for her sins, she had been dumped out of one of the palace windows by two eunuchs. Some of her blood had spattered on the wall, and on the horses below as the trampled on her carcass.

> "When they went to bury her, they found no more of her than the skull and the feet and the palms of the hands." (2 Kings 9:30-35)

King Joram (or Jehoram) – another one of Jesus' relatives – had married Athaliah, who proved to be the evil daughter of reprobate parents, Ahab and the infamous Jezebel. As a result of their perversion, the genealogist on whom the author of Matthew's Gospel was relying had skipped three consecutive kings of Judah who were themselves seen as especially degenerate and who were associated by birth with the cursed bloodline of Ahab. The list takes up again with one of the worthy ancestors of Jesus - Ozias or Uzziah.

This King Joram also turned out to be a truly evil ruler. On his way to the throne, he killed six of his brothers and later murdered the princes of Palestine. He was responsible for the invasion and plunder of Palestine by the Philistines, the Arabs and Ethiopians, and came to a bad end.

> "And after all this the Lord smote him in his bowels with an incurable disease. In the course of time, at the end of two years, his bowels came out because of the disease, and he died in great agony. His people made no fire in his honour, like the fires made for his fathers...He departed with no one's regret. They buried him in the city of David, but not in the tombs of the kings." (2 Chron.21:18-20)

King Ahaziah or Ahaz whose mother was Athaliah (daughter of Jezebel and grand-daughter to Omri and wife of King Joram) had walked in the ways of Ahab his father-in-law. His mother had been "his counsellor in doing wickedly" (2 Chron. 22:3).

> "He even burnt his son as an offering, according to the abominable practices of the nations...and he sacrificed and burned incense on the high places, and on the hills, and under every green tree" (2 Kings 16:3-4).

King Manasseh, like King Ahab before him, had also committed the heinous offence of erecting altars to the service of Ba'al. He had sacrificed his own son, practised sooth-saying and augurs and dealt with mediums and wizards (2 Chron. 33 and 2 Kings 21:2-6, 16). His son, King Amos, had been decadent and evil just like his father, slaughtering his own slaves and worshipping pagan gods (2 Chron. 33:21 ff and 2 Kings 21:20-21).

As the composer of Matthew's Gospel tell us, Jesus had an untidy bloodline of male ancestors with mothers and wives of suspicion, as well as five women who were questionable in their own right.

The presence of these five women in Jesus' bloodline is a fact very strange in itself since Semitic tribes and families, and people from many other nations besides, traced their forebears exclusively through the patriarchal line. The male members of any Jewish family, and particularly a first-born son such as Jesus, were keen to establish the status of the family and to assure the continuation of its property rights. When it came down to basic family and property questions, women were superfluous in Jesus' culture.

But more interesting still is the story behind each of these five women. All five were outsiders – and none with a clean slate. All irregular. The leaders and believers in the early church do not seem to have been nearly as prudish and pretentious as modern Roman Catholics in tracing a pure, unsullied, virginal line for their hero. No virgins in his genealogy. His origins, according to the early believers, were sullied, and some of his forebears proved to be characters of questionable reputations – though they were, after all, only characters out of the Old Testament – not top rank heroes and heroines of the New Alliance who were thought to be on the verge of virginal perfection.

As her story is told in the Book of Genesis, Tamar had been an adulteress. She had married Judah's wicked, first-born son, Er, whom God had slain before he could produce an heir. Tamar then married Er's brother, Onan, but he refused to engage in any productive sexual concourse with her because then he would 'know that (*according to the law*) any offspring would not be his'. So 'when he went into his brother's wife, he spilled his semen on the ground'. (Here we have the biblical origins of disapproval of masturbation and *coitus interruptus* – a passage much quoted in the moral manuals of the Roman Church.) God slew Onan, and Tamar went home to her father's house as a sterile widow and adulteress – a female with a troubled past.

Rahab was a foreigner from the kingdom of Jericho, and a harlot. She had given sanctuary to the two spies whom Joshua had sent out to investigate the area, and was therefore a liar to the king and a traitor to her own people by seeking to trade protection for her family in exchange for her silence and co-operation. She was a shadowy character.

Ruth was also a foreigner, from the land of Moab, and the daughter-in-law of Naomi. Both were widows and, when Naomi decided to return to her home in Bethlehem, Ruth was determined to go with her. So they went back to Bethlehem and tried to survive there together, as impoverished widows. A rich relative of Naomi met Ruth scavenging food in his field and showed some generosity towards her. With encouragement from her mother-in-law, and a few female tactical manoeuvres of her own, Ruth joined forces with Boaz and lived happily ever afterwards.

> So Boaz took Ruth and she became his wife; and he went in to her, and the Lord gave her conception, and she bore a son. They named him Obed; he was the father of Jesse, the father of David. (Ruth 4:13,17)

Matthew also included in his list the wife of a foreign mercenary, Uriah the Hittite. Her sordid story appears in 2 Samuel 11. When King David saw the beautiful Bathsheba, the daughter of Eliam, from the roof of his house, bathing naked, he was overcome with lust and sent his messengers to summon her. They lay together and she fell pregnant. To cover up the fruits of his adultery, David tried to give the Hittite warrior the opportunity of sleeping with his wife, but as an act of solidarity with his battle-hardened troops, Uriah slept at the door of David's house with the servants.

> The ark of Israel and Judah dwell in booths; and my lord Joab and the servants of my lord are camping in open field; shall I then go to my house, to eat and to drink, and to lie with my wife?

After one other similar attempt to entice Uriah to indulge himself with Bathsheba, David wrote a letter to Joab, the commander of his army, sealed it and handed it to Uriah to deliver.

> Set Uriah in the forefront of the hardest fighting, and then draw back from him that he may be struck down and die.

When David's order had been carried out and Uriah, the courageous Hittite, had been slain in the front line, the commander sent a message to his king to let him know.

> When the wife of Uriah heard that her husband was dead, she made lamentation for her husband. And when the mourning was over, David sent and brought her to his house, and she became his wife, and bore him a son.

From this unholy, adulterous alliance, the internationally famous king Solomon was born, and further down the genealogical line, 'Jesus was born, who is called Christ'. Without doubt, Jesus had a tainted blood-line.

The fifth woman in the genealogy was Jesus' mother, who appears elsewhere in Matthew's Gospel at various stages of her son's life. Mary was by far the most important figure in his early life and she was there at the end with a loyal band of female followers on Calvary.

A simple maiden, found to be with child, according to the story, before she and her husband had come together. At one stage, Joseph had thought to put her away, presumably because his future wife's expected child was not his. All the advice about daughters and wives in *The Wisdom of Jesus ben Sir*, in Philo's and Josephus' writings and in *The Sentences* of Pseudo-Phoclydes comes to mind. We have no idea whether Mary's father was ever told of her predicament, and if so, what he had thought of his little daughter. And we aren't told what transpired between Joseph and his spouse. What could she say? The story was true. Pregnant outside marriage. Just like the wayward daughters in the wisdom literature and like the other four women in Jesus' genealogy, her reputation was sullied. In recording his genealogy, the author of Matthew's Gospel was making a number of obvious, but important points.

First, like other important Jewish figures, Jesus had a genealogy that could be traced back to Abraham, and like other great Jewish leaders, King David, for example, there were serious irregularities in his heritage. Yet despite their shady records, they were all chosen by God to be part of his plan of salvation. As a son of Abraham, Jesus was a genuine Jew.

Second, his genealogical line was unusual. Not the standard, acceptable line identifying heroes and men of honour. Some of his forebears had been evil, degenerate men involved in pagan worship, in cruel, licentious misdeeds. And among his ancestors were a number of unconventional figures. He had family ties to four (or five including his own mother) women with suspicious pasts, each of whom was central in the Jewish debate about the Davidic messiah. These women were caught up in 'irregular' marital situations reflecting the state of affairs between Mary, Joseph and the Spirit, and yet they were all agents of God's messianic plan.

Thirdly, even his genealogy made Jesus a counter-cultural figure whose patriarchal line was contaminated by foreigners and women.

Fourthly, from the beginning of his Gospel, the author of Matthew was associating Jesus with Gentiles and sinners – with outcast of society.

And finally, maybe his genealogy was another way in which Matthew's author was trying to annoy the Pharisees and the legal fraternity – the people who demanded strict compliance with the law – the ultra-orthodox of the Jewish fraternity.

Luke's narrative also records a Jesus genealogy, one ascending from Joseph all the way to Adam rather than descending, as Matthew's does, from Abraham to Joseph; a genealogy with some names also found in Matthew's, but not many. The author of the Matthew Gospel artificially arranged Jesus' genealogy on the basis of the number 14 as he pointed out in Matthew 1:17. Some have suggested that this arrangement was probably based on the numerical value of the consonants in the Hebrew version of King David's name. While the Matthew version of the genealogy contains 42 names, the Lucan version has 77 named forebears, arranged in eleven tranches and culminating with God having the super-perfect number 77. David comes in at 42, being the end of a list of 6 tranches each of 7 names. Seven was regarded as a classically sacred, magical number.

Luke does not mention any female in his extended list. A curious fact since, in telling the story of Jesus, Matthew's Gospel, compared to Luke's, gives women only a minor role, whereas in Luke's narrative, women feature often and strongly, right from the beginning when, as Luke told the story, the angel appeared to cousin Elizabeth, and then to Mary.

Women of the Infancy Narratives

The story of the birth of Jesus is so well known it does not need repeating. What is less known is that the Christmas story as we know it is an amalgamation of the different narratives recorded by the authors of the gospels of Matthew and Luke, with some extraneous, legendary material added to the basic 'facts' as told in the gospels. While Mark's and John's gospels are silent on the important events surrounding Jesus' birth, there is little in common, little crossover between the infancy material in Luke's Gospel and that in Matthew's. As we have seen, even the genealogies are different – Matthew tracing a line from Abraham to Joseph, and Luke tracking a different line backwards from Joseph to Adam, passing through some common names such as David, Jesse, Obed, Boaz, Jacob, Isaac and Abraham.

Matthew's infancy narrative focuses on Joseph and Jesus. Nothing about the appearance of an angel to Mary. An angel does appear three times in a dream, but to Joseph. Matthew was clearly concerned to establish for his Jewish readers that the puzzling Old Testament prophecies had found their target in the appearance of Jesus on the world stage.

Unlike Luke's, Matthew's author did not go in for any preamble. He began with Joseph discovering to his great surprise that the girl in his life, his fiancée, was expecting, and continued the story with a dream in which an angel put his mind at rest with the news that Mary was pregnant by the power of the Spirit, and that he, Joseph, would name their son 'Jesus' (which is not what Luke reports).

Matthew tells us that the couple were 'betrothed', which might mean in our parlance something like engaged, or committed to one another and making plans to live together. Maybe they had signed a 'prenuptial' contract, a *ketubbah*, though it is impossible to know now how popular these contracts were, especially among the poor or the working class in a village to the north. Our modern ideas about marriage don't translate easily into ancient social practices, for in those days the union of two people was arranged by the respective families. Property passed hands, a dowry was provided, and the marriage was effected by a public agreement to live together, to engage in sexual concourse and raise children, by the girl leaving her family home and going to live with her husband and his family. It would appear that apart from the possibility of the prenuptial contract, none of these steps had been taken when the angel appeared to Joseph to explain Mary's pregnancy.

The Matthew scene then changes to Bethlehem in the days of King Herod, to the wise men who had arrived in Jerusalem from the east under the guidance of a star, and to Herod's plot to engage these men to find the child who had been prophesied to be a threat to his rule. They found the child 'with Mary his mother' in a stable, bestowed their mysterious, symbolic gifts and decided to ignore the king's request to return with news of the child's whereabouts.

Matthew's Gospel then recounts the story of Joseph's second dream and another angel's appearance, and the story of the little family's flight into Egypt, again to fulfil a prophecy. According to the story and to fulfil another prophecy, innocent male children in and around Palestine were slain. Then another dream and a third appearance of an angel, leading to Joseph bringing the family back out of Egypt and settling in Nazareth, in answer to another prophecy.

With details gathered from eyewitnesses and ministers of the word, the author of Luke's Gospel tells a different story. The principal figures in his narrative are female – Mary and her cousin Elizabeth – together with two babies (Jesus and his cousin John the Baptist), plus the angel Gabriel who appeared to Elizabeth's husband, Zechariah, and later to the young maiden Mary.

Luke's author spends some time on the story of the wondrous and mysterious conception of John the Baptist since Elizabeth had been past child-bearing age, and then describes a long meeting between his father and an angel in which Zechariah was instructed to name his son 'John'. Six months later, the same angel appeared to Mary in Nazareth, to a maiden betrothed to a man whose name was 'Joseph'. He greeted her, announced that she would conceive a son and that she (not Joseph) would name him 'Jesus'. He also told Mary of her cousin's good news, and after a brief conversation, Mary bowed humbly to the angel's proposal and set out on a journey into the mountains to visit Elizabeth.

In this part of the Luke's narrative, the events taking place, and the words spoken by the players – by Mary, Gabriel and Elizabeth – pointed to the momentous and mysterious significance of the conception of this child. The author of Luke constructed, in vivid detail, though in summary form, two meetings: Mary and the angel; Mary and her cousin. These conversations (as they are recorded) seem stiff and formal, full of literary, scriptural references and theological motifs. They project a sense of theatrical artifice. Legends in the making.

> An angel appeared to the maiden and said, 'Hail, full of grace, the Lord is with you!'... And he said to her, 'do not be afraid, Mary, for you have found favour with God. And behold, you will conceive in your womb and bear a son, and you shall call his name Jesus. He will be great, and will be called the Son of the Most High; and the Lord God will give to him the throne of his father David, and he will reign over the house of Jacob forever; and of his kingdom there will be no end.' And Mary said to the angel, 'how can this be, since I have no husband?' And the angel said to her, 'the Holy Spirit will come upon you, and the power of the Most High will overshadow you; therefore the child to be born will be called holy, the Son of God.'

A long journey followed. When Mary arrived at Zechariah's house and greeted her cousin, Elizabeth became ecstatic. A meeting of two women, both mothers-to-be, both playing a role in God's mysterious plan.

And Elizabeth shouted out,

'Blessed are you among women, and blessed is the fruit of your womb! And why is this blessing given me that the mother of my Lord should come to me? For behold, when the voice of your greeting came to my ears, the baby leaped for joy in my womb. And blessed is she who believed that there would be a fulfilment of what was spoken to her from the Lord.'

And Mary said,

'My soul magnifies the Lord, and my spirit rejoices in God my Saviour, for he has regarded the low estate of his handmaiden. For behold, henceforth all generations will call me blessed; for he who is mighty has done great things for me, and holy is his name. And his mercy is on those who fear him from generation to generation. He has put down the mighty from their thrones, and exalted those of low degree; he has filled the hungry with good things, and the rich he has sent empty away. He has helped his servant Israel, in remembrance of his mercy, as he spoke to our fathers, to Abraham and to his posterity forever.'

Women doing what women do – bearing children, giving birth to new life, to children as gifts of God. Two women being drafted by the Creator to be at the forefront of God's involvement in the world. Special women giving life to God's gift to mankind, feeding the tiny embryos in their wombs, delivering them into the world in a sealed bag, suckling them, cleaning them, protecting them from danger, teaching them to speak and to feed themselves, preparing them to take up their independent lives. How could Jerome or Innocent III or the monastic poets and the theologians of the Middle Ages speak of them in such pejorative and patronising tones! A slur on the Creator, on the female sex, and a monstrous distortion of Jesus' kingdom message.

The Luke Gospel goes on to tell the story of John's birth and his naming by his father Zechariah who was moved by the Spirit to prophesy in the words of an extended Eucharistic prayer. Difficult to imagine John the Baptist's father constructing this prayer off the top of his head. Another literary device.

The focus shifts to a faceless couple's journey up to Bethlehem to enrol in a Roman census; to Mary's delivery of her firstborn son – the swaddling clothes, the manger; to the shepherds and an angel appearing to them to announce the birth of a Saviour; to the sudden outburst into song of a multitude of heavenly hosts; and Mary keeping all these things, pondering them in her heart. More imaginative, legendary material. No mention of any wise men carrying gifts. Needless to say, there is some serious doubt about the census of Augustus, and even about Jesus' birth in Bethlehem, about the presence of angels and shepherds. These colourful details added theological flesh to the bare bones of a working-class birth.

Luke tells the story in a few words of the ritual removal of Jesus' foreskin and of his naming ceremony. A more expansive story follows – the story of the purification of the mother and her son in the Temple in Jerusalem and of a sacrifice offered – all prescribed by the Law of Moses. In the Temple, the family encountered Simeon who, according to the story, had words to say about the child and his importance to Palestine, and words to address to his mother. And we also meet an old prophetess, Anna. Yes, a female prophet who had lived years of her life as a widow in the Temple precincts.

In the Gospel of Luke, the author models his narrative of Mary's purification and Jesus' presentation in the Temple in Jerusalem on the story of Hannah and Elkanah as told in The First Book of Samuel.

Though she was well past the time of childbearing, Hannah had given birth to a son, Samuel. The author of Luke overlaid this basic story with a number of Gospel themes – fulfilment of God's promise of a Messiah who was his gift to all mankind (not just to Palestine but also to the Gentiles); Palestine's rejection of the Messiah; and the sorrow, the agony that was to flood over Mary his mother. Jesus' father and mother were stunned to hear what was being said about their little boy. Amazed by a message so unexpected, so puzzling.

The author was following his literary technique of pairing a male and a female in his narrative – Elizabeth and Zechariah; Mary and Joseph. He makes these pairs throughout his gospel: the widow of Zarephath and Naaman, the leprous commander of the army of the king of Syria; the sign of Jonah to Nineveh and the Queen of Sheba; the Pharisee and the publican, and an annoying, demanding widow; the healing of the demoniac man and of Peter's mother-in-law; the centurion of Capernaum and the widow of Naim; Simon the Pharisee and the sinful woman; the women at the tomb and the Emmaus disciples; and in Acts, Lydia and the jailer at Philippi. And here in the Temple, in the infancy narrative, Simeon and Anna the prophetess. Man and woman, Adam and Eve, Elkanah and Hannah, Joseph and Mary stand together, side by side in the world and before God. Equal in honour and grace, co-workers in the same vineyard.

According to the Mosaic Law, by virtue of the loss of blood involved in childbirth and because of a young mother's loss of her vitality in the birthing process, a girl like Mary was considered unclean after the birth of her son. Ritually unclean for seven days, just like any woman at the time of her menstruation, though if she had given birth to a female Messiah, Mary would have been unclean for two weeks. Obviously, in the Jewish culture (and in the Roman Church), boys were better than girls.

Furthermore, Mary had to be careful not to touch anything sacred, or to enter the sanctuary area of the Temple for 33 days, or in the case of female child, for 66 days. During the first seven days after birth (or fourteen for females), the mother's impurity was especially contagious, as dangerous as menstruation. These rules would constitute scandalous gender discrimination in today's legal world and, as we have seen in the case of the widow with a permanent haemorrhage, Jesus was not minded to endorse these laws for women.

Then once the mother's purification period had ended, she had to go to 'the door of the tent' (or to the Temple) to make her offerings – a burnt offering of a lamb and a sin offering of a young pigeon or turtledove, or alternatively, if she was poor, two turtledoves or two pigeons, one as a burnt offering, the other as a sin offering. The priest was commissioned to make these offerings before the Lord (and to receive his stipend), to make atonement to Yahweh for the mother. In this way a Jewish mother, Mary for example, was made pure again, cleansed 'from the flow of her blood'. From Luke's account we can conclude that Mary and Joseph regarded themselves as members of the poor fraternity since they only took two turtledoves to the Temple.

From the perspective of the twenty-first century, it's a little ironic to be reading about Mary's period of impurity during which she was forbidden to touch sacred objects or enter the sanctuary of the Temple for over a month, and during which, for seven days, she could contaminate anyone she came in contact with. She was after all the mother of the Saviour, the Messiah, the Holy One of God, touching him many times a day, changing his nappy, cleaning his bottom, wiping up his baby vomit, feeding him on her breast, rocking him to sleep. No wonder late in his life, Jesus was somewhat dismissive of these laws, man-made but given the terrifying authority of God by the establishment. Mary was living in two worlds, perhaps more.

Luke's infancy narrative concludes with the puzzling story of Jesus' unscheduled three-days lingering in the Temple at the age of twelve, at the end of the Passover feast. We have looked at this story earlier. His parents did not understand what he was supposed to have said in explanation of his disappearance. However, as Luke recounts, 'he went down with them and came to Nazareth, and was obedient to them; and his mother kept all these things in her heart.' And what the author of The First Book of Samuel said of young Samuel, the author of Luke repeats word-for-word of Jesus: 'And Jesus increased in wisdom and in stature, and favour with God and man.'

In the text, Samuel and Jesus are seen as mirror images, just as Hannah and Mary are in parallel. Mary's *Magnificat* prayer, her generous participation in the mysterious plan of salvation and her unquestioning obedience were pre-figured in the life of Hannah.

Luke and Matthew – two very different versions, almost no details in common. Two different readerships – one Jewish, the other mainly Greco-Roman. Two different theological perspectives – one focused on Jesus as the fulfilment of the Old Testament dispensation, the other consisted of the writings of a self-conscious *rapporteur* recording an orderly narrative, telling what had come down to him and others about the beginning of the Christian movement. The author of Luke's Gospel was setting out to establish a firm basis for the faith of his readers. He was stressing the physical and the spiritual blessings visited on both dimensions of God's plan – faith and giving birth, discipleship and motherhood. Two very different sets of *dramatis personae* – Luke stressing the role of women in the history of salvation. Women were central (Mary, Elizabeth, Anna). Their faith and co-operation were essential; the women speak, rejoice and praise God, while the male characters either remain silent like Joseph, are struck dumb like Zechariah, or long to escape like Simeon.

In the Lucan version of the infancy narrative, two women, Elizabeth and Mary, were the first to receive the message about the imminent arrival of a promised messiah. Both were praised and blessed by God's angelic messenger, and both were the first to sing and prophesy about the Christ child. Although in the contemporary culture (as we have seen in the resurrection narratives) the testimony of women like Mary Magdalene was not generally admissible or credible, these two women are depicted as the first witnesses of the events of John's and Jesus' births, and both were blessed with a central role in God's messianic plan.

In tune with one of the principal themes of Luke's Gospel, even before it was announced by Jesus during his public life, these two women are presented as the first example of God's policy of prioritising the lowly, the faceless, of reversing the 'normal' order in society and giving precedence to the poor, to lepers, to the downtrodden, to prisoners, to the publicans and rough shepherds – and to women.

Luke described Mary as a maiden, an unmarried girl, a virgin, a *parthenos*. He told his readers that the angel greeted her as 'full of grace' and, according to some ancient authorities, as 'blessed among women'. The messenger stated that God was with her, that she had found favour with him and was to become a mother by the power of the Spirit.

Contrary to the established custom and according to the author, this startled mother-to-be would have the privilege of conferring the name on the one whose kingdom would have no end. She was to be like the Ark of the Covenant in the desert where God's presence was powerfully focused among his people. 'The power of the Most High will overshadow you.'

In answer to the angel, Luke recorded that Mary described herself as the Lord's 'handmaiden' – literally his servant, his female slave. He presented this young girl as a model disciple answering God's call, surrendering herself, sacrificing her future, her social status and her relationship to Joseph, and falling into the hands of God. Like the fishermen and the tax collectors, she immediately left all things and followed God's call, a theme which Luke would take up in his gospel.

In Luke's narrative, God is seen to be turning his world on its head. The angel, the one who stood in the presence of God in Heaven, at God's throne, had come to a mountain village in Palestine, to visit an insignificant teenager and greet her as a person of high status. Luke's author clearly sought to establish in the mind of his readers how central, how pre-eminent this young girl was to the overall dispensation of salvation – an eyewitness, a participant, a model disciple, a woman of incredible faith. We read of the greeting she received when she visited her cousin. The child Elizabeth was expecting wriggled and kicked in his mother's womb. Filled with the Spirit, she proclaimed in a loud voice, as the angel had done, 'Blessed are you among women and blessed is the fruit of your womb! … And blessed is she who believed…'

Thrice blessed. Blessed because of her pregnancy, her motherhood and because she had this simple faith in God's promise. After Elizabeth had greeted her cousin with extravagant outbursts, the author has Mary launch into an ecstatic song of praise and rejoicing based on what God had gifted to her – a lowly servant girl, a faceless maiden, vulnerable and on the edge.

The praise song which the author put in the mouth of Mary was full of kingdom references was based on the song of Hannah, the mother of Samuel (1 Sam 20:1-11). The composer was portraying Mary and her cousin as replicas of an Old Testament prophetess who was forecasting the coming of the Messiah who was to be God's agent in accomplishing his plan. The third woman in the infancy narrative of Luke's Gospel, the elderly prophetess, Anna, who had lived her widowed life in the Temple in Jerusalem, in the shadow of the Holy of Holies, also spoke of the child Jesus to all who were expecting the messianic deliverance of God's chosen people.

Three couples feature in Luke's extended narrative. According to the story, the three women displayed an extraordinary trust in God's plan for them, a readiness to be involved, while the men (like the apostles later, and unlike the women in Jesus' life) hesitated, doubted, or sought to escape any involvement.

In the Gospel of Luke, Elizabeth was clearly more important than her husband, even though he was officiating as a priest in the Temple where his team (*Abijah*) was on duty. And Mary overshadowed her husband, Joseph. Both these women, contrary to custom, gave names to their sons – John and Jesus. And Anna, as old and weathered as she was at 84, is recorded as speaking of Jesus 'to all who were looking for the redemption of Jerusalem'. She was the second validating witness of the critical role this baby boy would play. As far as the author was concerned, her evidence was admissible among the Jews and Gentiles in the early church. Contrary to the limitations imposed on women in Jewish society, and more generally in the secular society, women were important to the author of Luke and in the new dispensation – participants, disciples, prophetesses, with a new-found freedom, equal to the male members of the community, at times pre-eminent, though it must be admitted that there is no sign in Luke's writings that he was rejecting the fixed structure of his patriarchal society. And as we have seen, Luke's composer didn't follow the lead of Matthew's Gospel and identify women as the first witnesses of Jesus' resurrection appearances.

Let us go behind the narrative of Luke's Gospel and reflect on the character who was graced to play her role on centrestage in his story.

A young girl from a village in the hills – Nazareth. Engaged to be married. We can assume she was a pious girl. No mention in the canonical literature of her parents, Anne and Joachim. They make their appearance for the first time in the *Proto-evangelium of James*, the apocryphal infancy narrative which dates from the middle of the second century and which was attributed (falsely, but in accordance with the literary practice of the times) to James, the brother of Jesus, who of course, had he had anything to do with the development of the text of the *Proto-evangelium*, would have known the names of his grandparents.

We don't know whether Mary had brothers or sisters, or whether she had been schooled outside her home, though in view of the status of women in those days, in that isolated part of the world, and because of the limited opportunities given to girls to learn, it is safe to surmise that this young girl could neither read nor write. On a number of occasions, the author of Luke tells us that she did not understand fully the events in which she had been involved – puzzling, pondering, as the apostles also did later on, searching for understanding. She was not from a family of high status – not a princess with an attractive dowry.

From this humble, unpromising material, the author constructed a portrait for his Christian readers of a well-mannered, sophisticated young woman who could burst into an original song of praise and thanksgiving modelled on a beautiful prayer of an Old Testament figure, who could agree to the most preposterous invitation from an angel, to change the direction of her life and become a prophetess, a believer, a model disciple and the mother of a messiah, of the saviour long expected. This is what the early church came to believe and what the author recorded.

The author of John's Gospel will also elevate this person to the status of a second Eve whom, as we have seen, her own son addressed as 'Woman'. In this Gospel narrative she was depicted as a central figure on the Hill of Skulls where Jesus was lifted up in his glory.

Apart from a passing reference to her during Jesus' public preaching ministry, the search for Jesus in Jerusalem when he was twelve years old as reported by Luke, her presence with her son at a marriage in Cana in John's Gospel and her presence in Jerusalem at the time of the Passover and Jesus' crucifixion, Mary disappeared into the background. Judging from the available records, no one can say with any confidence that she was a dominant figure in Jesus' adult life or in the life of the early church. No preaching. No miracles. No prophecies. No official ministry. No active participation in the life of the community, at least that we know of. Silence. The authors of our New Testament literature obviously did not feel the need to tell their readers, or to preserve a written memory, of Mary's continuing presence in the public life of Jesus and of the early church as it unfolded. Legend would later fill some of the gaps.

Women were present and prominent in Jesus' life and in his ministry and, for a time, in the life and structure of the early church, but not Mary. Apart from giving birth to Jesus and answering the angel's call with such grace, such faith, she was a figure mostly in the background, seldom visible, though significantly visible when she did make an appearance. However, it is surprising, perhaps shocking, especially to modern Catholic believers, that she is almost faceless throughout the Gospel documents.

It is a truism, but because of the institution's scandalous record in dealing with its female members, it needs to be made explicit that there is no reason to assert that Mary was not a real woman and a complete mother. Furthermore, because of the way this woman has been systematically removed from the world – supernaturalised, idealised, refashioned, glorified and theologised – we need to remember that Mary was a fully-fledged member of our human race.

A girl when she first responded to the angel, at an age when she would have been experiencing her first menstrual period and dealing with changes to her maturing body. (Sounds a little scandalous to pious ears and sensibilities. But it shouldn't be. To believe, to think, to say otherwise would constitute heresy). A mother giving birth to her first child as he squeezed out painfully along the birth canal, though legend would much later preserve her from birth-pains and deliver Jesus miraculously, painlessly, into the world, not via the vagina but by suddenly appearing like a genie out of a lamp. Breastfeeding, sleep-deprived, dirty nappies, a screaming baby. Life was tough for a time and in the story, the family was away from home, in Bethlehem, and later in Egypt.

Then gradually, a mature woman, sometimes puzzling over the strange behaviour of her gifted son. Stressed and shaking with anxiety and grief around the time of his trial and crucifixion. A woman, a female creature of God, a daughter of Eve before she became the mother of Jesus, a woman of faith, a disciple and a discreet participant in the ongoing and expanding life of the Church.

Then over time, as they did with Jesus, the Church and its theologians strove to surgically remove Mary's humanity, to suppress her womanhood, her fleshly reality, and to pretend that in fact she was a pure, sexless being, the Queen of Heaven, the Virgin of all virgins, immaculately conceived, perfect in ways other human beings could never hope to be. All other women might be inferior, second-class, weak, unreliable, unpredictable and a serious cause of temptation, but Mary was different. Special, in part because her womanhood had been removed. She was no longer part of that group. The Queen of Angels and Archangels. A Mystical Rose. Ark of the Covenant. A Virgin most Pure. No sparks between herself and her husband. No touching or back scratching. No kisses or holding hands. Separate bedrooms. A woman who, even as a girl, had successfully covered over, in public and in private, her feminine beauty and attractiveness.

The post-resurrection infancy narratives as told by the authors of Matthew and Luke do not provide any insight into how Jesus regarded women, how he engaged with them, involved them in his ministry or related to them. The stories hardly contain any details about how Mary related to her son, and certainly no details at all as to how Jesus, the central character of the stories, bonded to his mother. We have to wait for Jesus to grow to manhood, until he was 30 years of age and had embarked on his career, to address these questions. A man of the world mixing with his male companions and girlfriends.

However, this is not to say that the infancy narratives do not provide some insight, some understanding as to how the primitive Christian communities sought to present the role of women in the new dispensation that Jesus had launched. It is clear that both authors of the Gospels wanted their readers to know about the origin or the genealogical heritage of Jesus, and to read about the importance of women like Elizabeth and Anna, and especially the 'Woman', Mary, his mother. A woman was the central character in the begetting, the birth and education of the hero of their epic story. Her role was not to be forgotten as the authors went about recording the story of the turmoil and conflicts surrounding Jesus' public life. The primitive community in different locations wanted to know the details of the part Mary played, and to ensure that their memory of this 'Woman' would not drain away. She had welcomed the news of her pregnancy, nourished and protected the new life inside her body, given birth to a boy on a cold night in a stable (as the story goes), fed him on her young breasts, cuddled him in her arms, cleaned him, encouraging him to walk and talk, and answering his questions. I emphasise these mundane motherly, womanly, daily activities, which bonded Jesus to his mother, because they give the lie to the crazy argument of Thomas Aquinas and many others (even to the present day) that women cannot possibly be 'elevated' to the supernatural ranks of priestly ministry because by nature they do not share in the necessary pre-eminence reserved to a male. They argue that this pre-eminence allows men to touch the sacred vessels, to utter the words of transubstantiation, to hold the body of Christ in their hands, to forgive sins, to consecrate. According to them, women, by their nature, do not possess the status, the worthiness, the natural perfection necessary to exercise these frightening powers that can be entrusted only to men – to celibate men. These pious propositions are an affront to our common sense and to the story of Jesus. Women were touching Jesus from his birth, and ministering to him. Real touching. Intimate touching. Holding onto him. These basic facts reduce the prejudices of Aquinas and others to an unadulterated nonsense.

CHAPTER FOURTEEN

Telling It How It Is

True religion – what is it? What was it for Jesus the Prophet of God who, the gospel authors asserted, was bent on revealing the human face of God to the world?

Ceremonial and grace-filled signs; vestments and golden vessels; rules and petty regulations; dogmas and moribund traditions; male priests, bishops and important archbishops, sporting red patent-leather shoes with silver buckles and wearing chastity belts for the glory of God?

What did it mean for Jesus to be a religious person and to live a genuine religious life?

We know what it meant for the Jewish elite and the Pharisees. They imagined (or pretended) they were obeying the law of God and serving Yahweh, and were puzzled by the fact that God was not acknowledging their long prayers and their fasting. They complained, 'Why have we fasted and you don't even see it?' (Isa 58:3).

According to the prophet Isaiah, the fasts that God wanted to see were the daily deeds of those who loosened the bonds of wickedness, who let the oppressed go free, who smashed yokes and lifted burdens, who shared their bread with the hungry, who clothed the naked and invited the homeless to their house.

In a word, for Jesus (and for those other prophets who revealed God's secret to the world), religion consisted in living on earth the life of the Kingdom of Heaven rather than worshipping false gods and carrying on endlessly in castles constructed by men for their own glorification.

Jesus' God was not hanging around waiting to be honoured, looking for sacrifices, counting prayers and demanding satisfaction. And this mysterious Being was not standing by to answer pious petitions, (to increase our bank account or reward us with a good mark in an examination). Any decent god would not be the least gratified by a string of masses or even a monastery full of celibate monks chanting celestial songs. That god has long since left the building.

Jesus' God was a mysterious presence at the heart of our world who wanted his beautiful creatures to get on with their lives, to be their better selves, to live together happily and inspired by his spirit of generosity and transparency, with integrity and in peace. The Being Jesus was contacting in his prayer life had a kingdom that was 'coming' and a will that was 'to be done' here on earth. He wanted his men and women to celebrate their lives, to dance and sing together, to remember their blessings and to plan their future. Real, earth-bound stuff.

In preaching his message, Jesus often talked to his listeners in images that would have readily been understood by women. Those women who were used to spinning and weaving for their families would have pricked up their ears when they heard a street preacher enter their domestic world and speak of a creator who had fashioned the lilies of the field – glorious flowers which neither toiled nor spun, yet at the height of his glory King Solomon was not arrayed as one of them. The parable of the widow who had lost one of her little silver coins and was like God searching feverishly until he had recovered one of his children who was lost – this story would have elicited a knowing smile from any member of the country women's league in Nazareth or Bethany. Or the widow who was so annoyingly persistent in demanding her rights before the nonchalant judge. This storyteller could see the world through women's eyes, not merely from a male-oriented point of view. The image of the mother hen sheltering her chicks under her wing, or the cook who pummelled a pinch of yeast into her dough to bake bread for the household – Jesus was speaking to women in the crowd, talking their language, modifying and enriching the traditional image of God as a man, a father, a warrior, a shepherd, a king. Jesus' God was also like the poor woman searching for the coin, like the fussing mother hen. His God made the lilies of the field, and like a proud mother, she counted the hairs of her child's head.

As the two senior Australian clerics, dressed in flashy Renaissance gear, stood together overlooking the Square of St Peter, muttering to one another about the vast assemblage of dignitaries before them, perhaps they were theologically on the money to regard what they were seeing out there in the wilderness of the Vatican as a field of weeds. It might have appeared to the world that the Christian faith had burst out in all its glory in the Vatican precincts; but if we are to attend to Jesus' message, the genuine religious life is being lived out elsewhere, far away, in orphanages and prisons, in hospitals and schools for the poor, in hidden places and by faceless believers. The weeds of the parable were growing strong in the Vatican soil where men had taken charge, but the wheat was putting down its roots in the wetlands and marshes where believing women (and faith-filled men) were toiling.

In Jesus' lifetime, the priests, the scribes and Pharisees were the leaders in charge of administering the religious institutions, interpreting the law, preserving the system of beliefs and practices. But according to Jesus the Prophet of God, they were leading God's children astray, poisoning their minds and exploiting their powerful position for their own material benefit. And all of them were of the masculine persuasion.

Jesus travelled up and down the country, preaching, teaching, and revealing the secrets of the kingdom. No matter how hard he tried, his male disciples never really understood this kingdom message. The penny never dropped. They never got it. But the women seemed to understand – a range of different women with their own baggage to carry around: Mary Magdalene, the Samaritan woman, the pagan woman from Syrophoenicia, the widows and prostitutes, Martha and Mary, the women on Calvary. They got the message, but when the time came, they were never allowed to step forward to deliver it. They were systematically excluded.

The truth is we don't know exactly what Jesus was like – but then we don't know what anyone's like exactly. He didn't set out to tell us about himself. He wanted to tell us about the kingdom and how to participate. And his best friends didn't tell us about him either, or his enemies for that matter. Pilate was silent on the subject, and Caiaphas said nothing. Not a word from Peter his apostle, or James his brother, or Mary Magdalene his friend, or from Lazarus and his sisters. We only have what others wanted us to know – people who were forty or fifty years off the pace and who were reliant on the memories and impressions that had been preserved and handed down. Though the Gospel records are mixed in, like the wheat and the weeds, with a range of theological motifs, they are more than likely reasonably accurate – or at least not wildly inaccurate. Those who had known Jesus (or knew someone who had known him) would not have tolerated the publication of any grossly disfiguring caricature of such an important religious figure. I am confident that what I have written about Jesus and his relationship with all kinds of women, accurately describes a significant dimension of the man who appears in the Gospel literature.

If we can believe the sources, Jesus was not anxious or on guard in the presence of women. He did not involve himself in issues of impurity or veiling, or restricting women to their domestic domain, or demanding that they be seen in public only when accompanied by a male relative. The Jesus we meet in the Gospels acted without concerning himself with the rules and regulations. His was an uncomplicated freedom that erupted out of a heart untouched by cultural or religious scruples.

Jesus didn't look at women and see a source of temptation or ritual contamination. He treated them with respect, dignity and compassion. He spoke about serious issues with them and revealed to them important features of himself and his mission. He didn't hesitate to welcome them as his students, his disciples, or as part of his special group of followers. They journeyed along with him and his friends. Never a word of criticism or disrespect. Never a put-down such as he directed towards the scribes and Pharisees, or expressions of annoyance such as he sometimes addressed to his dull-witted male followers. We have no evidence that he advised them, as Paul would do, that they should be submissive to their husbands or wear the appropriate headdress, and he never spoke about female seductiveness, their fickleness, their unworthiness and natural sinfulness as the Fathers of the Church would do. He reversed the classical view of the male and female role in any illicit sexual wrestling. The major factor in those encounters was not a woman's seductiveness, her behaviour, her presentation, but man's sheer lustfulness: 'I say to you that everyone who looks at a woman lustfully has already committed adultery with her in his heart' (Matt 5:28).

While mixing with men and attacking the establishment, Jesus was still able to maintain a high level of deep spiritual intensity, to foster a life of prayerfulness and to preserve his contacts with the world of women. A strong, uncompromising man, but through all the weariness, the loneliness, the disappointments, the heartache, he was also a man who was sensitive to the world of women.

Jesus was not your average rabbi, or your standard prophet. For anyone familiar with Jewish society of the period, it is a shock to realise how Jesus mingled with women in private and on the public stage. They were attracted to him. They were there listening to his preaching and following him around. They spoke to him, and he to them – friends, followers, disciples, pagan women and prostitutes. Nothing like this has been reported elsewhere in Palestine's literature or the early Christian writings. He used to associate with the elite of Jewish society, and with the dregs of society – the sick and the lame, sinners and outcasts, lepers and the unclean, tax collectors and loose women. For Jesus, a communal meal was a foretaste of God's kingdom and he used to eat with all kinds of unworthy people, publicans and sinners. These were the people, the hated tax collectors and the local harlots, who would be first in the kingdom he preached, before the chief priests or the elders.

Some simple folk and popes are content to say that women have always been excluded and that's the end of it. It's our tradition, and our tradition enshrines the will of God and reflects the mind of Jesus – we cannot change it. That's the way it has to be. Just get over it, and get on with preaching the Gospel.

It's true that women have never enjoyed any real power in the Church. But as far as I can see, Jesus never founded a church. A church was the last thing on his mind. He was interested in promoting a kingdom – a world of inclusion and equality, of freedom, of love and mercy, of service to the poor and oppressed – a world in which women would have an important part to play. They were his faithful disciples, his friends, the ones he commissioned to announce the good news of his new life among them. They had understood his message. They were members of his inner circle and playing off the bench in his A-grade team. They have not been very visible in the institution, it's true, but as far as I can see, an institution was not on Jesus' agenda. He was not constructing another institution to rival the Jewish establishment. He had been called to create a new world for all members of the human race.

Knowing the story of the Catholic Church and its scandalous treatment of women, of what has been said about them over the centuries by monks, theologians and other dignitaries, it may come as a surprise to a modern reader of the gospel literature when her attention is focused on the women who were coming in and out of the Preacher's life: those he loved, the ones he ministered to, those whom he involved in his work, the ones who followed him, the ones who believed in him, the women he helped and supported, those he recognised and dignified, the ones in whose company he relaxed. There were women in his life: Mary Magdalene whom he loved more than any of the apostles; Mary of Bethany and her sister Martha; Salome; the feisty Syrophoenician woman; the sensual sinner who washed his feet at the feast while the other exclusively male guests watched in amazement (and probably with a tinge of envy); the old lady who had summoned her courage and touched him in the street; the widow wrinkled with age who had crept into the synagogue on the Sabbath; Peter's mother-in-law; the widow of Nain (Jesus seemed to have had a magnetic attraction which drew widows to him); the poor woman who had been sprung in the act and was facing death by stoning; and of course, his mother and her cousin Elizabeth.

Unfortunately – for some in the Catholic Church – women are everywhere. It would be easier for the reactionaries if it were otherwise. But women now have a voice. They are visible and educated. They occupy positions of power in society: prime ministers, presidents, lawyers, doctors, university professors, High Court judges, jockeys and horse trainers, astronauts and board members, journalists, novelists, poets, thinkers, shearers and union leaders – but, for heaven's sake, not priests, not popes. Perish the thought. They might be inclined to undermine the power structure, ask tough questions, challenge the incumbents, pour scorn on the unspoken code of clerical behaviour and the cosy club regulations, insist on a return to Jesus' idea of religion, look to the future and scuttle Peter's ocean liner. And perhaps Jesus would cease weeping.

What Say You, Christine de Pizan?

And yet, whoever's said or written ill
Of woman, only good is said of them
In books that talk of Jesus, of His love,
Or of His death pursued so jealously;
The Gospel says no ill of them, but all
Record their high responsibilities,
Great prudence, great good sense, great constancy,
Their perfect love, their lasting faithfulness,
Their ample charity, their fervent will.
With firm and steadfast heart and mind they longed
To serve the Lord, as they indeed did show,
For never did they leave him, live or dead;
Except for women was sweet Jesus left
Alone completely, wounded, stricken, dead.
In just one woman all the faith remained.
How foolish is the man who sullies them,
If only for the reverence due to her,
The Queen of Heaven, in remembrance of
Her goodness; so noble and dignified,
She earned the right to bear the son of God!
(lines 557-576)

Christine de Pizan,
Letter of the God of Love,
1399 AD

Bibliography

Primary Sources

The Gospel of Mark
The Gospel of Matthew
The Gospel of Luke
The Gospel of John
Paul's First Epistle to the Corinthians

Bible translations

I have used the RSV for the majority of scripture quotations. Scripture taken from the *Revised Standard Version*, Grand Rapids: Zondervan, 1971. Where I have used the original Jerusalem Bible I have indicated so in the text. From *The Jerusalem Bible* © 1966 by Darton Longman & Todd Ltd and Doubleday and Company Ltd. Where I have used my own translation or a paraphrase I have indicated so with an asterisk.

Secondary Sources

Reza Aslan, *Zealot: The Life and Times of Jesus of Nazareth*, Allen & Unwin, 2013.

Jacques Duquesne, *Jésus*, Editions J'ai lu, Flammarion, 2011.

John R. Meier, *A Marginal Jew: Rethinking the Historical Jesus, Volume 1: The Roots of the Problem and the Person*, Doubleday, 1991.

—, *A Marginal Jew, Volume 2: Mentor, Message and Miracles*, Doubleday, 1994.

—, *A Marginal Jew, Volume 3: Companions and Competitors*, Doubleday, 2001.

—, *A Marginal Jew, Volume 4: Law and Love*, Doubleday, 2009.

Jose Antonio Pagola, *Jesus: An Historical Approximation*, trans. by Margaret Wilde, Convivium Press, 2015.

Charles Perrot, *Jésus*, Que Sais-je? series, Presses Universitaires de France, 3rd Edition, 1998.

Roger Poudrier, *L'Insoumis de Nazareth: Les Controverses de Jésus avec les Autorités*, Médiapaul, 1999.

Christiane Rancé, *Jésus*, Gallimard, 2008.

Ernest Renan, *Vie de Jésus*, Edition établie, présentée et annotée par Jean Gaulmier, Gallimard, 1974.

Geza Vermes, *The Changing Faces of Jesus*, The Penguin Press, 2000.

—, *Jesus the Jew: A Historian's Reading of the Gospels*, Fortress Press, 1981.

Ben Witherington III, *Women in the Ministry of Jesus*, Cambridge University Press, 1984.

—, *Women and the Genesis of Christianity*, Cambridge University Press, 1990.

Gospel References

The woman caught in adultery: John 8:1-11.

The foreign woman at the well: John 4:1-42.

Two sisters at home: Luke 10:38-42; John 11:1-44.

A female admirer: Luke 7:36-50; Mark 14:3-9; Matt 26:6-13; John 12:1-8.

The Syro-Phoenician woman: Mark 7:24-30; Matt 15:21-28.

The woman ritually impure: Mark 5:21-33; Matt 9:18-22; Luke 8:40-48.

The widow's temple donation: Mark 12:41-44; Luke 21:1-4.

Chaos in the synagogue: Luke 13:10-17.

An ambitious mother: Mark 10:35-40; Matt 20:20-23.

Jesus' female followers: Luke 8:1-3.

The women of the passion: Mark 15:40-41; Matt 27:55-56; Luke 23:49 and 55-56; John 19:25-27.

The farewell supper: Mark 14:12-25; Matt 26:14-29; Luke 22:3-20; John 13-17; 1 Cor 11:23-25.

The post-resurrection stories: Mark 16:1-20; Matt 28:1-20; Luke 24:1-53; John 20:1-17; 1 Cor 15:3-8.

Jesus' family tree: Matt 1:1-17; Luke 3:23-38.

The infancy narratives: Matt 1:18-2:23; Luke 1:5-2:52.

www.ingramcontent.com/pod-product-compliance
Lightning Source LLC
Chambersburg PA
CBHW070346240426
43671CB00013BA/2424